# The College of Obscure Knowledge

## A LIGHTHEARTED LOOK AT AN ODD COLLECTION OF TRIVIA

by
Jim Marbles

Trade Life Books
Tulsa, Oklahoma

*The College of Obscure Knowledge:*
*A Lighthearted Look at an Odd Collection of Trivia*
ISBN 1-57757-017-0
Copyright © 1998 by Jim Marbles
P.O. Box 552
Tulsa, Oklahoma 74155

**2nd Printing**

Published by Trade Life Books
P.O. Box 55325
Tulsa, Oklahoma 74155

# INTRODUCTION

Welcome to *The College of Obscure Knowledge!* We are delighted
that you have decided to enroll in our unique college full of fascinating,
fun-filled facts, information, details, and insights about life's most baffling
mysteries! Jim Marbles delivers the straight talk on the most-requested queries
from radio's popular "College of Obscure Knowledge." Marbles, a well-known
radio personality tackles readers' most compelling questions with tons of research
and humor.

This is the best part! No tests. No pop quizzes. No papers. No class attendance. No
tardies. And no boring lectures! Just learning for the sake of FUN!! Simply open
this book and begin reading to savor this collection of the most popular
and most requested topics from the first decade of *The College of
Obscure Knowledge*. And, oh yes—

HAVE A GREAT TIME!

# The College of Obscure Knowledge

## A LIGHTHEARTED LOOK AT
## AN ODD COLLECTION OF TRIVIA

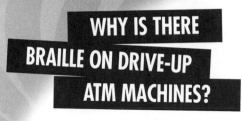

## WHY IS THERE BRAILLE ON DRIVE-UP ATM MACHINES?

Simple answer: all the machines are made the same . . . whether for indoor or outdoor (drive-through) use.

But since we are in the business of OBSCURE knowledge, betcha didn't know we owe the origin of the ATM to Dallas Cowboy legend and sportscaster "Dandy Don" Meredith. Yup. He and brother Jack Meredith founded Docutel in 1969 and started the whole thing.

Betcha also didn't know the machines shine a light through each bill to make sure two are not stuck together, so you don't get too much dough. Now I'm sure you comedians will ask about that seeing-eye dog sign on store doors. (Just WHO is that sign for anyway?)

*The College of Obscure Knowledge*

In trying to find an answer to this question, we ran across an interesting legend we have not heard before . . . and judging from the requests received for copies of the legend, not too many others have either!

The legend has it that on the way to the Crucifixion, a bystander was indentured to help the beaten and tortured Jesus carry the cross. Named Simon of Cyrene, tradition has it that he was an egg merchant and returned home to find his hens had laid eggs in a rainbow of colors.

**WHY DO WE COLOR EASTER EGGS?**

This early legend, combined with the ancient's reverence of eggs as a symbol of birth and life, easily moved into our celebrations when the Church began to celebrate the Resurrection in the Spring.

# IS IT TRUE THE 4TH REALLY ISN'T INDEPENDENCE DAY?

The first image that comes to mind is the powdered wigs and knickers as everybody lines up to sign the Declaration of Independence like in the famous paintings.
Nothing could be further from the truth.

The year is 1776. June 7th, the motion is made and 33-year-old Thomas Jefferson writes it. A few changes later and July 2nd, the Second Continental Congress adopts it. The next day, July 3rd, it is published. July 4th, a partial vote. July 8th it is read aloud from the balcony at Independence Hall. July 9th it is read aloud to Washington and his troops. Also on July 9th, New York votes on it. Any of those days could be our holiday. We just settled on July 4th.

Interestingly, most of the signers had affixed their signatures to it by August. Yet, more than a half dozen held off till much later. In fact, Thomas McKean played it safe and waited until the year 1781. Some who voted for it never signed it. But strangest of all, the original copy of the Declaration is missing! It was last seen at the printer early morning on the 5th. The copy on display is the only original with signatures!

9

The College of Obscure Knowledge

Well, the name was! Monsanto, the chemical company, came up with Chemstrand—nylon fibers woven into a polyester backing, similar to a toupée (you know that thing guys wear on their head!), as a grass-like artificial turf.

It was really expensive. One exclusive prep school in Rhode Island used it in a field before sports arenas ever heard of it.

Then came Texas billionaire Judge Roy Hofheinz who built the Houston Astrodome in 1965, with a 5,000 panel glass roof. Problem was, you couldn't play ball due to the glare, so the dome was painted over. Then the grass died. They were desperate for an answer. One year after opening the Astrodome, the infield was de-turfed and Chemstrand put in. It worked great! Monsanto, seeing the opportunity of a lifetime, renamed the stuff "Astroturf," and the rest is miniature-golf surface history.

Currently, the Astrodome has three miles of zippers holding together over 14,000 square feet of Astroturf!

## WAS ASTROTURF REALLY INVENTED IN THE ASTRODOME?

10

## WAS THERE REALLY A RIDE BY PAUL REVERE?

Yeah, kinda. The poem by Henry Wadsworth Longfellow is as loose with the facts as a Hollywood adaptation of a novel.

Revere was an interesting fellow—much like Jefferson. He was a Renaissance man of many talents. You know about the silver smithing. He also was an inventor, did engraving and iron foundry, and was an artist. He was also a patriot. He took part in the Boston Tea Party and made several horseback rides to relay information.

The ride of April 18th that is immortalized in prose was actually a wake-up call to John Hancock and Samuel Adams in Lexington. On the way, he roused the countryside by yelling, not the British are coming, but THE REGULARS ARE ABOUT!

He never made it to Concord that night. He even missed the Battle of Lexington while getting a trunk Hancock left behind. He did get paid five shillings for his efforts. Obscure ironic fact: The grandfather of the aforementioned Henry Wadsworth Longfellow tried to court-martial Paul Revere for cowardice during the Revolutionary War.

The Birthday Song is as old as the hills— the Hill Sisters, that is.

In 1893, sisters Mildred Hill and Patty Smith Hill wrote a cute little kindergarten ditty called "Good Morning to All" with the tune we all know as "Happy Birthday to You." The lyrics were changed to "Happy Birthday to You" in the roaring 20's and published without permission. A third Hill sister, Jessica, brought in the lawyers when the tune appeared in 1933 in a Broadway play. We're positive it wasn't for the money, but for the memory of Mildred who had been dead 17 years by then.

## WHO WROTE THE BIRTHDAY SONG?

Anyway, Jessica won! To this day royalties are paid to the Hill sisters. Not to be confused with the Hills Brothers who instead of royal-teas prefer royal coffees. Get it? Royal-teas!

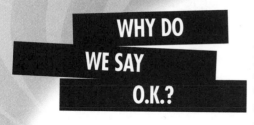

# WHY DO WE SAY O.K.?

The College of Obscure Knowledge

Nobody knows.
Nobody can agree. A hundred different stories for this common expression of approval have come to light, and here are just a few of them:

Some say it is of ethnic origin. Some say it may be from the Surinam *okee*, or perhaps the Jamaican *oh ki*, or the Choctaw *okeh*—all having about the same meaning: "It is well" or "It is so". Some support the fad theory. Through the 1830's and 40's, East Coast newspapers began abbreviating sayings and phrases, much like the presidential initial fad of the 60's. O.K. for *oll korrect* was the only survivor of this fad. Spelling improved, too, I see.

Some attribute *oll korrect* as a reference to the backwoods schooling of Andrew Jackson. Which brings us to the most agreed-upon theory: O.K. stands for "Old Kinderhook", a nickname for Martin Van Buren in the 1840 presidential election.

What's this fascination with the word *nine*? Well, at least here, we have something to go on.

The word *yards* is the key, and the cause of controversy as well!

Did the original saying refer to cloth? One source says it takes nine yards of fabric to make a suit and that the term came from the tailoring industry. No one agrees with that idea. A caller to the radio show suggested the whole nine yards means a first down in football. The problem is that the saying predates the game.

## WHY IS IT THE WHOLE NINE YARDS?

Another caller suggested it might be a nautical term on a sailing ship. Gary Hudder, concrete expert from Chandler, Arizona, confirmed our suspicion that the whole nine yards may refer to concrete delivery. Ready-mix trucks average nine cubic yards: the whole nine yards would be a full order—at least in the old days.

Obscure fact: Mr. Hudder reminds humanity, you build with concrete. Cement is glue.

14

## WHERE DID WE GET THE PHRASE EAT CROW?

Human beings get themselves into the greatest trouble with their mouths. What we say and how we say it denotes our stations in life, our breeding, and our attitudes. The New Testament book of James is full of warnings about the tongue.

Throughout history, people have had to eat their words which led to sayings such as "eating your hat" to "eating humble pie."

The best story is from Charles Earle Funk in his book, *Hog On Ice*. During the War of 1812, a British officer came upon a Yankee soldier who had just shot a crow. The British officer complimented the Yankee on his gun, asked to see it . . . then, at gunpoint, forced the Yankee to take a bite out of the crow. After a reprimand, the British officer gave the gun back. The Yankee, now with the gun, forced the Brit to finish the crow. Later, the Yankee was asked if he had indeed seen the British officer. He reportedly replied that he had dined with him yesterday.

15

*The College of Obscure Knowledge*

An interesting fact for all you dieters . . . the wind-chill factor is based on calorie counting!

Calories are the body-burning energy that keep you warm. If you lose calories due to wind blowing them away, you feel colder than the air outside. It's like being in a cold river—the water steals away your body heat. The good news is that wind-chill has no effect on inanimate, unfeeling objects like cars, houses, tractors, or your boss at work!

## HOW IS THE WIND-CHILL FACTOR MEASURED?

The opposite of the wind-chill factor is the heat index. Those who live with high humidity are acquainted with those times when the body can't evaporatively cool efficiently. In plain words, the heat index measures those times when sweat doesn't evaporate on the skin to cool you down.

Obscure fact: The only difference between sweat and perspiration is three syllables.

## DOES ALUMINUM IN MOBILE HOMES ATTRACT TORNADOES?

No. I live in tornado alley in Oklahoma. I spent my college days in West Texas. Over the years I have learned the basics: if a tornado is coming, go to a small, enclosed room in the center of your home (bathtubs have saved a lot of lives), stay away from windows, pray hard, promise to start tithing, and seek shelter if you are in something that isn't nailed down.

Why? Simply put, mobile homes are fragile, rarely adequately anchored, and usually can't withstand over 100-mile-per-hour winds—a mere F1 on the tornado scale. A tornado can rally to the force and speed of an F5 on the Fujita tornado scale. Tornadoes are not attracted to aluminum in mobile homes and trailers. They are simply too forceful for a mobile home or trailer to withstand.

Obscure fact: You are safer in a hole, ditch, or culvert than in a mobile home during a tornado.

It's the human equivalent of feasting at a banquet table versus being spoon-fed strained spinach.

Dogs have a keen sense of smell. They can pick out a certain scent and track it down much like a human can hear a certain noise and follow it to its source. Hanging out a car window is a banquet of smells for Rover—new, exciting, and dangerous! And, with no sweat glands, dogs love the breeze. However, when you inhale whatever air is around you and your dog, process it through your lungs, and expel it out your foul-smelling mouth in a narrow, concentrated burst into your dog's face . . . anyone would snap at you and try to bite your fool nose off!

**WHY DOES A DOG LOVE TO HANG HIS HEAD OUT OF THE CAR WINDOW— BUT HATE IT WHEN YOU BLOW WIND IN HIS FACE?**

Not-so-obscure fact: Letting your dog face off into the wind in your car is not a good idea. Besides the obvious slipping or jumping, ear infections could result, and bits of sand, debris, or even bugs could damage your dog's eyes.

## WAS THERE A MOTHER GOOSE?

We think so, though it is a fascinating mystery . . . .

The stories and folklore surrounding Mother Goose date back to 1697 with the French publication of a collection of fairy tales (not to be confused with Nursery Rhymes) written by Charles Perrault (not to be confused with the CBS on-the-road correspondent) in which Mother Goose is pictured. This original book contained such familiar stories as "Little Red Riding Hood". Now the story gets strange. Ten years before any English translation of the Perrault book, a man named Thomas Fleet published *Mother Goose's Melodies for Children* in Boston in 1719. Fleet's mother-in-law was Elizabeth Foster Vergoose, who reportedly had sixteen children, ten of them adopted.

These people really existed. The book was published, but no copy of it has ever been found. If you find one, it would be worth millions . . . not counting my 10 percent finder's fee! The 1790 Newberry of London publication of *Mother Goose Stories and Rhymes* is the one that made the name familiar to this day.

19

I'm sure this is a line from George Carlin. But the more you think about it, you wonder . . . .

Teflon is short for polytetrafluoroethylene. It is used in everything from plumbing (that thin white tape you put around threads) to bullets (so they won't hurt as much?). It is put on frying pans much the same as the finish is put on your car—starting off with bare metal, roughing it up with grit, putting on some primer, and so on.

## HOW DO MANUFACTURERS GET TEFLON TO STICK TO NON-STICK PANS?

After primer, three baked-on coats of Teflon get applied, and wha-la! . . . no more sticky eggs.

20

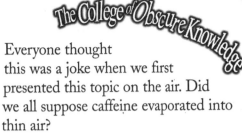

The College of Obscure Knowledge

## WHAT DO THEY DO WITH THE CAFFEINE AFTER THEY TAKE IT OUT OF COFFEE?

Everyone thought this was a joke when we first presented this topic on the air. Did we all suppose caffeine evaporated into thin air?

Coffee manufacturers are making a bundle selling the caffeine they leech from the coffee! The method of removing caffeine from coffee beans, since being discovered accidentally has resulted in a secondary big business—something the coffee manufacturers really don't want you to know about! If you are wanting to rid caffeine out of your life, good luck! Not only are most Americans hooked on it through coffee, but caffeine is injected into a mass of consumer products as well. Check out any over-the-counter medication! A good percentage have caffeine, especially pain relievers and cold and allergy medications.

Obscure fact: Most Americans are loading up on caffeine—not with coffee, but with soft drinks and chocolate.

According to Richard Armour in the collection called *Light Armour* (1954):

Shake and shake the catsup bottle, none will come, and then a lot'll.

The term you like to use appears to be a matter of personal choice and/or snobbiness. The original *ke-tsiap* was from China. The English use the spelling *ketchup*. (But they also spell *gray* wrong.) Common, everyday usage in America is *catsup*. Gourmets say we hicks use ketchup. By the way, this is one of those words that the longer you look at it, the weirder it looks. Try it.

**IS IT CATSUP OR KETCHUP?**

Obscure fact: Tomatoes were thought to be poisonous until the 1800's.

Obscure fact for marketing purposes: Heinz says their ketchup/catsup is SO SLOW (how slow is it!?!) that it travels at 25 miles per YEAR.

# WHY DOES SKIN FORM ON HOT MILK?

FAT. Next question.
Oh, you want details!

It is similar to an oil and water mix for salad—they don't mix. When heated, the fat in the milk no longer mixes with the water in the milk. It floats to the top. Think of it as one big lava light. The fat hits the air and cools, and viola! SKIN. The fat is the majority of the flavor of milk.

Obscure fact: Gravy skin goes away when warm because of the starch melting.

Obscure impossibility: The one answer we can't find (and really don't want to) is who, or perhaps more importantly, WHY did adult humans start to drink milk?

Nope! Not Julius Caesar or Caesar Augustus . . . or any of those guys.

It is a recent invention. But we found conflicting stories. (Usually when that happens, it means that there is a grain of truth in each one and the rest has become legend.)

There is the story of a cook/restaurant owner Caesar Cardini of Tijuana, Mexico, who invented the dish of garlic-enhanced leaves of lettuce as an appetizer in the 1920's. The story goes that the dish was a hit with Hollywood celebrities who spread news of the dish up North.

Another story has the familiar salad named after Caesar's Palace in Las Vegas. Yet a third, and harder to believe, story has a restaurant patron not paying for her lunch and the proprietor yelling at someone to "seize her salad"! (I tend to believe the first story.)

Obscure fact: The term *salad* comes from the Latin *herba salata* meaning "salted veggies".

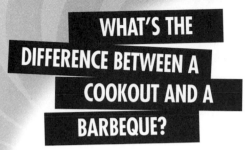

## WHAT'S THE DIFFERENCE BETWEEN A COOKOUT AND A BARBEQUE?

We here in the great American West tend to get snippy about our barbeque, just like we do our chili. Everybody agrees that the word *barbeque* comes from the Spanish *barbacoa* that originally referred to the grill of sticks they cooked on. Today, the word describes any kind of gathering in which a man that won't go near a stove considers himself an expert in burning animal flesh over petroleum-soaked briquettes in a suburban backyard.

Actually, barbeque is a process. Smokin' Joe Resnick of Oklahoma, the creator of the best barbeque (and jerky) in the universe, tells us it is a precise art involving choice meat, slowly smoked over hickory for many hours at a precise 200 degrees, and best left to the experts.

Obscure fact #1: Expert smoked meats have a smoke ring—a pink tint on the outside layers of the meat.

25

**The College of Obscure Knowledge** From ancient days to modern dishwashing commercials, "I can see myself in it!" has held fascination for all of us vain, but admittedly homely people.

The first mirrors were highly polished plates of metal, much like you can find in interstate rest areas. In Venice in the 1500's, someone noticed the shiny, reflective quality of mercury (like the silver stuff in a fever thermometer) and smeared some on a pane of glass. From then on, a mercury/tin coating on glass became the standard for hundreds of years.

## HOW DO THEY MAKE MIRRORS?

The 1800's brought the silver-type coating we have today; a silver ammonia mixture thinned down and applied to the back of glass. There was a problem with silver, as anyone who owns silver-plated anything knows. It tarnishes. That's why the stains exist that we find on old mirrors. Today, we use an aluminum/chromium film compound.

26

## WHY ARE TV'S BLACK AND COMPUTERS WHITE?

Home electronics seem to follow trends.

Remember when all stereo receivers and cassette decks were silver? Now they are all black. Early TV's were, for the most part, wood. Designed to be an upscale piece of furniture until they started getting affordable—entered plastic! Check out some of the early 60's TV's and you'll find white, chrome, and all sorts of stark-deco monstrosities to match that oriental furniture. Slowly, black began to dominate the TV scene, mainly because it goes with everything in any decor.

Early computers couldn't decide on TRS-80 gray or Commodore-64 tan. The industry seemed to settle on file cabinet off-white. In fact, first efforts at black monitors didn't work, because they looked like cheap TV's. Times are a changin'! With home computers proliferating, and competition intense, companies are trying new colors. Look for more black, some trendy teals, and Sony now has a purple PC!

Part of it is your imagination. Part of it is evaporation.

First, your brain. We learn in school, and it is fact, that a big part of taste is smell. The aroma of food combines with texture and taste to make you go YUM! If one of the three is foul, so is the enjoyment of whatever we are eating. If one of the three is overwhelming, we think it's the best thing since Mom's home cooking. Truth is, fresh baked, hot goods SMELL better, so we assume they TASTE better. That's why God put our noses right smack dab over our mouths.

**HOW COME COOKIES AND BREAD TASTE BETTER RIGHT OUT OF THE OVEN?**

Second, science. The starchy part of bread depends on moisture, and as bread cools, the water in it cools and evaporates, along with some of the flavor and texture. That's why a few seconds in the microwave enhance even stale baked goods.

## WHY DO DEER FREEZE IN HEADLIGHTS?

Because their mother taught them to.

In the wild, there are predators and prey. When faced with danger, each animal reacts with pure instinct. Predators size up the threat and either fight or bolt (much in the same way man does). Everything else has its own unique, God-given method of survival: turtles retreat into their shell, rabbits dart back and forth to avoid capture, possums play dead, and deer freeze. This self-defense mechanism works—with everything except cars. That's why turtles, rabbits, possum, and deer become roadkill. The predators—coyotes, big cats, and the like—if they have time enough, size up the situation, realize they don't know what they're dealing with, and hightail it outta there.

Obscure myth: There is a belief that Armadillos are born dead on the road. This is not true. Armadillos are poor-sighted, near to the ground sniffers, and react to motion, jumping to avoid danger. In other words, if a car's tire doesn't get them, the bumper will.

29

*The College of Obscure Knowledge* No, but no one can really agree on how many years a dog year is. In case we've lost you, we are comparing human years to the life expectancy of a dog.

In real life, a dog lives 10 to 14 years, depending on the breed. Humans have always wanted to know how far along Poochie was by comparing its age to a human's age. The common misconception of a dog living the equivalent of seven years in one calendar year was a dog food marketing ploy. A closer approximation would be anywhere from 4 to 6 years.

Here's why it's tough to figure: small breeds mature faster and live longer (we thought my parent's poodle would outlive us all). A dog reaches breeding maturity in 6 to 9 months (your human equivalent of a teenager wanting the keys). Shortly thereafter, it settles down (the human equivalent of a teenager discovering he has a brain). By 5 or 6, your dog is set in its ways, and a good companion (the human equivalent of wanting to be a teenager again).

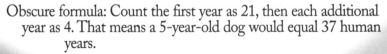

**IS A DOG YEAR ACTUALLY SEVEN YEARS?**

Obscure formula: Count the first year as 21, then each additional year as 4. That means a 5-year-old dog would equal 37 human years.

# WHY CLOUD NINE?

Because "Eight is Enough"?

This simple, everyday phrase gave us the most trouble of anything ever asked of "The College of Obscure Knowledge". No one knew the answer. We found no book, no reference. We finally found a mention in *Everyday Phrases* by Neil Ewart who theorizes the number nine, being a multiple of the lucky number three, was of special significance and the original saying was "cloud seven" or the common "seventh heaven".

We found this interesting—but unsatisfying. We have found old published clichés from the 1700's referring to the nines as the ultimate: "dressed to the nines" is a surviving example.

Obscure best-guess theory: Though the origin is lost in the sands of time, the phrase "the nines" was used like we use "the Ritz".

31

Middle ages are a matter of attitude. With some, it means a settling down. With others, it means a toupée and a red sports car.

Oops, wrong topic. You mean historically. Depending on which highbrow you talk to, the Middle Ages fall anywhere from 500 A.D. to 1500 A.D.—more or less anything between the end of Rome and the Renaissance. It is one of those times in history when we as humans didn't advance much. We had metal which produced swords and knives, we advanced to castle-like mortar structures, and stayed at that level, advancing little, inventing nothing, writing hardly at all for about a thousand years.

## WHAT'S THE DIFFERENCE BETWEEN THE MIDDLE AND DARK AGES?

When all the conquerors and bullies settled down, we had a Renaissance. That meant we stopped fighting for a few minutes and thought about things. The intellectuals of that period called the previous few centuries the Dark Ages. The Christian church was the only stable society during the entire period. Fortunate for us, the clergy preserved knowledge and literacy.

Obscure fact: The term *medieval* refers to anything in the Middle Ages. (That's why turning 40 seems "ieval".)

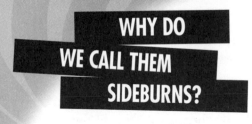

## WHY DO WE CALL THEM SIDEBURNS?

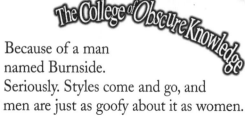

Because of a man named Burnside. Seriously. Styles come and go, and men are just as goofy about it as women.

If you think old yearbooks are funny, check out Civil War era facial hair fads. All the Army generals look like characters from "Spinal Tap". Full beards were the norm, handlebar moustaches were common, but one guy surpassed them all by shaving his chin while leaving the rest of the beard. His name? General Ambrose E. Burnside. He is described as being dashing and flamboyant, and his hair style, not to mention that cute face, started a trend. A play on his name leaves us with the label we have today. Don't laugh. After a less-than-stellar war career, Burnside later became governor of Rhode Island, then a U.S. Senator.

Obscure truth: Hair, clothes and, beard fads (e.g., goatees) are for the young so they can look back at pictures years later and ask themselves, "What were we thinking?"

There was once—
in the mid forties.
What happened?

Perhaps we lost it during the war effort. Perhaps aliens landed in Roswell and demanded it for themselves. Perhaps the government needed the room. The last answer is correct. (Though number two is my favorite theory.)

Obscure insight: Betcha didn't know. TV and FM radio are on the same frequency band. But each broadcast TV channel takes up hundreds of times more space on the FM band than your average FM radio station. Channel One is 44-50 megahertz. Your favorite radio station is probably 94.5 or 100.9 megahertz. See the difference? You could put something like 40 radio stations in that room!

## WHY IS THERE NO CHANNEL ONE?

Needing the space, even before FM ruled the airwaves, the FCC (the Federal Communications Commission) allocated that bandwidth for mobile radios.

## WHERE DID THE RUDOLF AND THE RED-NOSED STORY ORIGINATE?

Like a lot of Christmas gifts, we got this story from Wards. Seriously!

The year was 1939. The Montgomery Wards in Chicago wanted something besides candy for Santa to hand out to holiday shoppers. Ward's ad man Robert May took a friend, Denver Gillen, to the zoo to study deer. Gillen sketched a cute little guy, and May wrote a neat little poem called Rollo, the Red-Nosed Reindeer.

The head office liked everything but the name Rollo. So the name Rudolf was adopted. (The name is said to have come from May's four-year-old daughter.)

The Christmas handout was used for about ten years. During that time about 2,500,000 were distributed. Robert May had some good luck with friends. Another buddy, Johnny Marks, set the poem to music, but no one really noticed until Gene Autry recorded it in 1949. Of course, the rest is history.

Obscure fact: At last count, 80,000,000 copies of the song have sold.

No, not really.

The inventor of the first pancake mix, Charles Rutt, was desperate. He had a great idea, but needed a marketing strategy. He especially needed a down-home, wholesome name. We can only hope he wasn't calling them Rutt cakes or something like that. In 1889, Charles went to a blackface vaudeville show. In the show was an actor, singing a tune called "My Aunt Jemima". Inspired, he turned the image into the loving image of quality he needed.

## WAS THERE EVER AN AUNT JEMIMA?

Obscure fact: At the Chicago World's Columbian Exposition in 1893, visitors were introduced to what the Davis Milling Company touted as Aunt Jemima. She had served over a million pancakes by the time the festival was over. She was actually recruited to play the part. In truth, she was really Kentuckian Nancy Green, a cook for a Chicago judge.

## WHY DOESN'T ANYONE EVER SMILE IN OLD PHOTOGRAPHS?

Actually, there are several reasons, and one theory. The theory is my favorite. Here are the reasons: Real early photography took a long time for exposures. Remember how uncomfortable your last family portrait was? Think of sitting in Victorian clothes with no air conditioning for a 10- to 20-minute exposure! Sitting for a photo was like sitting for an oil portrait. Unless you were one of the rich and famous (like grinning Teddy Roosevelt), it was a big deal.

The photographer was reminding them that this is for posterity, as opposed to the modern "this is for the yearbook!" You never know when your photo is being taken (and there are hundreds of you in just that one outfit you hate).

The theory as to why no one smiled in old photographs: bad teeth.

When first asked this question, I thought, Here is one that will involve months of calling to find the right person, only to be hung up on when they think I'm a "crank". To my everlasting delight, I found the answer in no less than two different sources! And they both agree! (Which probably means one got it from the other.)

The *New York Library Book of Answers* says the average McDonald's burger is 1.6 ounces. The Quarter Pounder is 4 ounces, bringing us to an average 3 ounces times 3 billion. Grand total: 560,000,000 pounds of beef a year. Cecil Adams in *The Straight Dope* has that exact figure, but goes further. Assuming 12 percent to 15 percent of the edible part of the cow is made into hamburger, that leaves 100 pounds of meat per cow, arriving at the astronomical figure of 5,600,000 cows. We believe that number to be too high. With an average of 500 pounds of meat per cow, processing would be cheaper to just grind the whole thing into hamburger.

## HOW MANY COWS DOES McDONALD'S PROCESS IN A YEAR?

Obscure fact: Speaking of cows, it takes 3,000 cows to supply the NFL with a season's worth of footballs.

## WAS THERE A REAL ST. NICHOLAS?

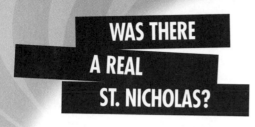

The College of Obscure Knowledge

Yes. Actually, there was more than one. There was a Ninth Century pope named St. Nicholas, but the folklore and legend surrounded Nicholas of Lycia, a Fourth Century bishop of Myra in Asia Minor.

Nicholas was orphaned as a child, dedicated his life to Christianity, and became a young bishop. He was imprisoned by the Roman Emperor Gaius Diocletianus and freed by the Emperor Constantine. Nicholas was a member of the Council of Nicaea in 325 and is thought to have died in 342. Those are the facts—the rest is the fun stuff!

Nicholas is said to have stilled a sea storm, making him the patron saint of sailors. His generosity and fondness for the little ones was legendary. To this day, St. Nicholas is said to have lived on—with his long white beard and red and white bishop's robes and miter headwear, riding a donkey, and delivering gifts to kids on or near Christmas celebrations.

The Dutch called St. Nicholas *Sinterklass*, which has evolved into Santa Claus.

39

For the same reason they lick their fur. They like to keep tidy and clean—and dry. In the wild, cats don't hesitate to swim (where do you think that taste for fish comes from?). Even domesticated cats will go for a fish if the opportunity is right (they sometimes insist on an outboard on a 20 footer with 20 pound test line). Dogs will play in mud and roll around in who knows what, but cats would rather not get messed up, because then they would have to clean up.

The main reason is: water has texture, and to your house cat, texture means substance, and that just means some substance they would have to lick off, doing tongue aerobics until everything is just right. A house cat's idea of working is jerking upright when they hear the can opener.

**WHY DO CATS HATE WATER?**

Obscure fact: Cats DO always land on their feet—if they have enough time to flip—due to advanced inner-ear equilibrium.

More obscure fact: In 1880, a cat fell 160 feet down the shaft of the unfinished Washington Monument—and was not seriously injured.

## WHAT ARE THE MOST AGGRESSIVE DOGS?

New York City did a study over 27 years on the worst biting offenders. So, not counting cabbies, politicians, and talk show hosts, here are the breeds with the highest number of biting incidences: The Worst Biting Dogs—German Shepherds (German police dogs), Chows (often found in junkyards), Italian Bulldogs, and Fox Terriers.

Obscure fact #1: The book called *The Intelligence of Dogs* says the smartest dog is the Border Collie.

Obscure fact #2: The dumbest dog is the Afghan Hound.

Obscure fact #3: The heaviest dog on record was a 310 pound St. Bernard (think of the slobber on that puppy)!

This Christmas tradition of the Mistletoe has nothing at all to do with Christmas.

This amazing green parasite can suck the very life out of its "host", much like some relatives during the Holiday! High priests gathered it from sacred oaks. It was hung outside to welcome travelers and inside as religious decor. Even enemies meeting under a mistletoe-infested tree were to lay down arms. That tradition evolved into kissing whoever stood under it.

**WHAT ABOUT THAT PARASITE THAT HANGS AROUND THE OFFICE: NO, NOT HIM . . . I MEAN MISTLETOE!**

Now a spray is cunningly hung over a doorway or place of vantage beneath which the romantic "mistletoe kiss" may be claimed. A berry is plucked after each kiss. When the berries are gone, the privilege of kissing ceases.

42

# WHAT'S THE STORY BEHIND APRIL FOOLS?

A day just for pranksters has been around forever. The Romans called the day (in Latin): *festum stultorium* (which, coincidentally was the real name of the deputy on *Gunsmoke*).

The modern day fooling around is said to have originated in France when King Charles IX proclaimed New Year's Day be moved to January 1st. Old timers, not liking the change, continued to celebrate on April 1st, and were the victim of ridicule—to the point of receiving invitations to bogus celebrations. These die-hards were called poisson'd Avil or April Fish.

FISH?!? (You'd think snaild' jour or something!)

Obscure fact: Evidently the time—being under the astrological sign of Pisces—prompted the name-calling "April Fish."

43

The flaming red poinsettia plant is now familiar to the Christmas season. It's hard to image that the poinsettia was unknown to us until the early 1800's.

The plant is named after our first Ambassador to Mexico, Dr. Joel Roberts Poinsett, who found the plant south of the border called "flower of the blessed night" due to either the resemblance to the star of Bethlehem, or the peak of color near Christmas. He sent some plants home, and they loved it, and named it after Dr. Poinsett.

## HOW DID POINSETTIAS BECOME A CHRISTMAS TRADITION?

Obscure fact: It is not a flower, but a tree—a spurge to be exact.

Obscure literary fact: The correct pronunciation is poin-set-ti-a, though we in the West tend to drop a syllable.

Obscure governmental fact: Contrary to rumor, the plant is not poisonous to humans as determined by the U.S. Consumer Products Safety Commission in 1975. (No word on how they tested it.)

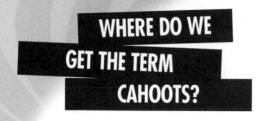

## WHERE DO WE GET THE TERM CAHOOTS?

They're spread when you touch hands. You get rid of them when you wash your hands. . . . No, I'm sorry—that's cooties!

The sources we found agree on this item! No different stories here, no sir. In fact, al printed material on this goofy Southern-sounding word is amazingly identical to each other—meaning one must have gotten it from the other. Here, we distill the literary prose into a meaning everyone can understand. You might say we are "in cahoots", meaning we are on the same team, or both up to the same mischief.

Sources say the word is of mediaeval Germanic origin *kajuetes* meaning a shack. Huh? Well, evidently robbers, rascals, bandits, and bad guys in the Black Forest of Germany would get together in their *kajuetes* as sort of a boys' clubhouse and plan out their exploits.

Obscure in-case-you-asked fact: *Cooties* come from the Polynesian kutu meaning lice. Just makes you itch thinking about it. . . .

**The College of Obscure Knowledge** There go those rascals in advertising/marketing! They have a way of making everything seem better than it is. Why do you think gas prices end in point nine?

In a perfect world, TV's would be marketed as a 17 "by 22" instead of a 27 inch. But there are a couple of reasons they are not: part of your TV tube is covered with the frame of the cabinet. As televisions age, the actual viewing size shrinks, but due to the frame around the tube, you probably don't notice it. In fact, in Canada, the actual tube size is required on the box. Check it out.

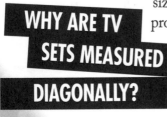

# WHY ARE TV SETS MEASURED DIAGONALLY?

Obscure fact: The real reason we measure televisions diagonally—televisions all used to be round. There was no other way to measure them. Old TV's—take a look at them!

# WHY DOESN'T THE RADIO STATION PLAY MY REQUEST?

Ah . . . I remember the good old days. Each town had one or two stations. One played rock, one played country. And the D.J.'s had a stack of records and a library to choose from. All we needed was your call to tell us what song to play.

No more. Now, every song is carefully programmed and preselected and played in order. Why? Due to FCC ruling in the 80's, every city now has perhaps 30 signals to choose from. Every station must choose a format, just like every restaurant must choose the type of food they serve.

In a city of any size, you can bet that every song is carefully selected to attract and hold a listener. Every song has been tested and programmed in with that in mind. Except for specialty request shows, your chance of hearing a request is virtually nil.

47

Hey, you listeners never look like we expect either!

After years of facing dropped jaws upon first meeting those on the other side of the radio, we've come up with the answer. It's just another way TV and movies are affecting our lives.

On the screen, big or little, the voices match the face. If they don't, they don't get the job. Goofy looking people get goofy looking voices—ala, Steve Erkel.

**WHY DON'T D.J.'S EVER LOOK LIKE WE EXPECT?**

On radio, many of the announcers are hired sight-unseen. Most important: their voice. So when you hear those smooth, deep, resonant voices, your mind automatically dials up whatever actor or actress the voice reminds you of.

Just remember, when you hear your favorite announcer in real life faces and voices don't automatically match up!

## WHY ARE BARNS RED AND HOUSES WHITE?

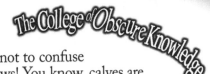

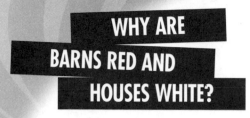

So as not to confuse the cows! You know, calves are always hearing, "Shut the door! Were you born in a house?"

Actually, it was pioneer ingenuity. You had to protect the wooden structures from the elements or risk losing it all to picture framers who covet old barn wood. So, without the local paint shop close by, they mixed a concoction of lime, linseed oil, iron oxide, and a handy commodity—milk. The iron oxide gave barns that rust-red color. The milk gave it strong bones.

Houses are white out of tradition mostly. The Puritans painted everything white. Big, old grand homes modeled after classic architecture are always white, an example being the Southern plantations and that house in Washington, D.C. I forget the name.

White goes with everything, suggests cleanliness, and is always in style. Now, can we please outlaw that salmon pink that keeps showing up in subdivisions!?

Obscure fact: Realizing white reflects heat (colors absorb heat), more and more public vehicles like school buses are painting their roofs white.

49

I know, nothing is more frustrating— except trying to guess the amount of gas in an outdoor grill. The easy answer is: there is no accurate way of measuring how much gas is in your gas tank. Even gas stations use a ruler to measure the amount of fuel in their underground storage tanks!

Here's the deal: your car's gas tank is very much like the tank sitting on the back of your home toilet. The float and arm wired to the dashboard gauge give an electronic, approximate reading of where that float is sitting. Now, here's the kicker: you can fill up the tank enough to submerge the float! It's as high as it will go, so you see a FULL indication in the dash. You have to burn off a good amount of fuel to have the float . . . ah . . . float!

## WHY DO GAS GAUGES LINGER ON FULL, THEN DROP LIKE A ROCK?

Obscure fact: Carmakers make sure the float stops before you are empty, since we all seem to run dry between paydays.

# HOW DOES A MICROWAVE OVEN WORK?

It makes mindless little things get all excited and jump all around. So, you're thinking, it must work just like professional wrestling. Sure.

The appliances actually use microwaves—super-high frequency radiation (SHF-like radar waves) generated by an electron tube called a magnetron with a low-tech fan spreading the waves. It's the fan you hear when the thing cranks up. The waves cause water molecules to vibrate. The vibrating produces friction. Friction-heat is kind of like large thighs in corduroy. That's why foods, with their moisture content, heat up while plates and paper do not.

Obscure fact: What's the difference between a 600 watt oven and a 1000 watt oven? About a minute—when it comes to boiling a cup of water.

It happens every Thanksgiving! Everybody wants that tender, wide slice of white meat and all that's left over are those stringy chunks of dark meat. At least that's what I'm told happens at the big table. Us kids at the card table eat what we can get!

Every bird, be it turkey or chicken, duck, goose or hummingbird, has both white and dark meat. Some have more of one kind, another more of the other. We call the difference, "Lifestyles of the Fowl and Famous!"

## WHY DOES FOWL HAVE BOTH WHITE MEAT AND DARK MEAT?

I could go into details about myoglobin and muscle fabric, but I just ate some nuggets. Fowl that fly, such as ducks and geese, have more dark meat. Those who don't fly except on holidays and during fare wars, such as your chickens and turkeys, have large areas of white meat. Only legs are dark.

Obscure insight: Simply put, hard-working muscles are dark, and the rest are white.

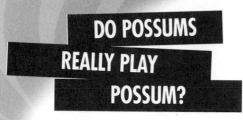

## DO POSSUMS REALLY PLAY POSSUM?

Yes, in dire circumstances.

Possums will hiss and try to use their sharp teeth if cornered. But if faced with certain death from a predator, possums will faint dead away into a self-induced coma. Some experts think it may be a shock reaction akin to fainting goats. No amount of poking or prodding will snap them out of it until danger is past unless, of course, you toss the possum in water! That will show you if you have a dead marsupial on your conscience or not.

Obscure fact: Possums have as many as 20 young a year, so tiny at birth they could all fit into a thimble. They are, indeed, marsupials—like kangaroos, keeping young in a pouch.

I think this scene has bothered all of us at one time or another and caused us to wonder why a fish floats upside down.

No, it isn't wanting its tummy scratched. The reason is basic biochemistry. Upon going to its eternal reward, the fish's stomach and other internal organs tend to collect air and decomposing gases, which naturally ascend upward. So the fish flips and floats.

## WHY DO FISH FLOAT UPSIDE DOWN WHEN THEY DIE?

Obscure fact: Most fish don't sleep, at least sleep as we know it. Although there are periods of lowered activity, fish don't need a bedtime story.

## HOW ACCURATE IS THE GROUNDHOG IN PREDICTING WEATHER?

Not accurate at all.

The groundhog can no more predict the weather than my teenager. This largest member of the squirrel family (the groundhog, not my teenager) may have its name as a Dutch translation of aardvark. The *New York Library Book of Answers* places the groundhog at 28 percent accuracy in weather prediction in the last 60 years.

And in case you are wondering, the groundhog comes out of its burrow driven by two primordial instincts: love and hunger. These are the only reasons he comes out of his burrow.

Obscure fact: The original German legend used a badger in the role of weather predictor. But, finding no badgers in Pennsylvania, the settlers used the groundhog instead.

To get technical about it, certain foods have an amino acid named tryptophan which aids serotonin which helps us sleep. If the names sound familiar, it is because the terms have recently been thrown about as controversial sleep aids.

Now the real story. Though turkey and dairy products have tryptophan, it's probably not enough to explain why your Uncle John became comatose in the recliner. Humans all have a tendency to want to sleep right after noon.

## WHY ARE WE DROWSY AFTER EATING TURKEY?

This fact, coupled with the fact that your body and brain know that you don't have to work that day, and the fact that you just stuffed yourself silly at a card table sitting on a folded chair, makes any available couch a deathtrap.

Why does this affect mostly men and not women? Traditional roles keep the girls talking in the kitchen, the guys settled at the TV in the den.

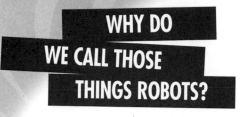

## WHY DO WE CALL THOSE THINGS ROBOTS?

From that cheesy robot on "Lost in Space" with the dryer vent arms, to R2-D2, to Commander Data, robots have come a long way. Though far from perfect in real life, robots come alive in TV and movies. Yet, the stage is where they were invented.

Step with me into the time machine to the roaring 20's. The industrial revolution had changed society. World War I had just been fought with machines. New inventions were popping up every day, and creative types saw it coming.

Enter: Karl Capek, a Czech who wrote a play named "R.U.R." about mechanical workers rising up against humans who created them (note: this same theme is in the Terminator series 60 years later). Capek used the Czech word *robota* meaning "oppressive work" and shortened it to *robot*. The play fired the imagination of a changing world spawning such movie classics as Fritz Lang's "Metropolis" released in 1927 (available now on video).

57

Any book on literary phrases or clichés has this listed, and none can agree. But we located some great stories!

Several say the term *charley horse* was commonly used to describe a horse—perhaps an old swayback with its better years behind it. Some say charley was a nickname for a night watchman, kind of like we use cop. Yet two more sources expand this thought.

The story goes that in 1640, Charles I of England greatly reinforced London police with new recruits. In dubious honor of his majesty, they called them charleys. They had no mounts, and their tired feet gave rise to the phrase. That would be like Americans calling FBI men hoovers.

## WHY IS A LEG CRAMP CALLED A CHARLEY HORSE?

Another great story is there was a workhorse named Charley who endeared himself to fans at the Chicago White Sox ballpark. Of the two reports on this poor animal, one said he had a limp, the other said any leg pain the players suffered made them empathetic to the worker/mascot.

58

## HOW DOES THE WEATHERMAN MAGICALLY APPEAR IN FRONT OF A MAP?

The process is called chromakey.

Simply put, it substitutes a color for an image. The weatherman stands in front of a large colored screen or wall, and they substitute that color for a map, video, or cute picture of little animals frolicking in the outdoors. As you may have guessed, they have to be careful to use a color the weatherman is not wearing, or you will imagine those x-ray specs you ordered from the comic book really work. Usually the color is a weird fluorescent blue or green—a color not seen on the normal human.

I once saw Jim Varney, who plays the character Earnest, wear a shirt in the chromakey color and appear on our local TV with our weatherman. It appeared like parts of him were missing as he screamed, "Hey Vern . . . help me! I got video disease!"

First, I would like to thank those who made radio possible: James Clark Maxwell of Scotland, Heinrich Hertz of Germany, Lee De Forest of the USA and of course, Guglielmo Marconi originally from Bologna, Italy, then of England—having moved because he had his fill of Bologna. (Sorry.)

Ever popped open the back of your old transistor radio and oo-aah-ed over all the circuitry? Quick and simple history of technology: big old tubes gave way to little transistors, and those transistors are giving way to tiny chips. That's why your cell phone doesn't weigh 30 pounds. Another innard in your radio is the filter capacitor. It's sort of a voltage regulator, and once it's powered up, it goes, plugged in or not, until the juice is drained away by the transistors.

## WHY DO I HEAR SOUND OUT OF A RADIO AFTER IT'S UNPLUGGED?

Ah radio. What a marvelous invention!

60

# WHY ARE PENNIES AND NICKELS SMOOTH AND OTHER COINS SERRATED?

First you have to realize that coins used to be really worth something, and we are not talking inflation here. We are talking real silver. Don't go smelting down your change though. There has been no silver in U.S. mass-produced coins since 1965. But during the old gold standard days, you were assured you could trade your money for gold, and the coins in those days weren't too shabby—90 percent silver in some cases.

As a result, a dishonest person could whittle a little off a coin and pile up some excess silver. Serrated edges put a stop to that.

The nickel was introduced in 1866. It was 75 percent copper and 25 percent nickel which were considered cheap ingredients like the penny. As a result, no anti-filing edge was needed.

Obscure fact: It takes 2.59 cents to make a nickel and 1.42 cents to make a dime.

Simple answer: blue veins run deep.

When you blush, the red blood surfaces near to the skin where we can see its redness. Those bluish veins are blood seen through lots of skin and hardly any light—making red blood appear blue. (I ran across a scientific description of oxygen feeding hemoglobin, then losing oxygen to turn a pretty teal-colored deoxyhemoglobin.)

Obscure fact: You are no doubt familiar with Royals being called blue bloods. This interpretation is of Spanish origin because the aristocracy had such blue veins:

**WHY DOES RED BLOOD LOOK BLUE UNDER THE SURFACE OF YOUR SKIN?**

Translated: they had fair skin.

Translated: they didn't get much sun.

Translated: they didn't work (just sat around all day reading romance novels about an earlier, more romantic era).

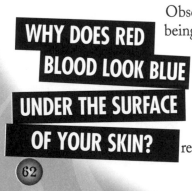

62

## WHY ARE COWS SACRED IN INDIA?

Bet you thought this one was easy, huh? Religion and all that. Well, that's just the half of it.

There is a legend in India of Prithu, a god who took the form of a cow to encourage his believers to be vegetarians. There are similar Greek and Egyptian stories. In India, influences from Buddhism and Jainism led to the belief that even a fly could hold a human soul, much less a cow, where there is much more room.

Modern day Hindus revere the cow as the symbol of motherhood and the source of the five sacred products of the cow: milk, curd, butter, urine, and dung.

Obscure fact: The urine and dung are used for medicinal purposes, and—like the cow patties in the pioneer days—for fuel.

There are two main reasons: support and decoration.

First of all, support: when a pig is roasted to perfection, the meat is tender and flakes off with a fork. Some gourmets want the ventilation shaft that used to be a mouth open during cooking, so they prop it open with a block of wood, rock or whatever. An apple would just roast away to mush after a couple of hours. After cooking, they insert a fresh apple.

**WHY DO WE PUT APPLES IN ROASTED PIGS' MOUTHS?**

Which brings us to reason number two: decoration. Not only roasted pigs, but everyone looks fetching with apples in their mouths, cranberries in their eyes, and flower leis around their necks.

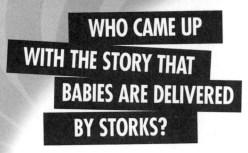

## WHO CAME UP WITH THE STORY THAT BABIES ARE DELIVERED BY STORKS?

The College of Obscure Knowledge

We can trace this back to Hans Christian Anderson, who expounded on an old folk legend to bring the story to life in his children's tales in the Nineteenth Century.

The stork, which encompasses as many as 17 different kinds of birds, is common in the Old World, but only one type is found in America. In Europe, and where the legend originates, in Scandinavia, the storks' favorite nesting sites are chimneys. Rather than a nuisance, it was considered good luck to have the quiet stork choose your home for its home—giving credence to the legend of delivering a precious package.

Obscure fact: Just hope the stork didn't feed you on its way to deliver you. It's a scavenger, and also enjoys frogs and mice.

For the same reason you punch your pillow, smooth the sheets, and turn down the comforter. They are getting ready for bed, and wanting to be comfortable.

We spend our lives trying to undo a dog's basic instincts, except those which we think are entertaining or cute, provided they don't tear up anything. The circling is similar to the cute little digging with the front paws your dog does right before a nap on that discarded coat. Don't you think a lump in his side makes for uncomfortable sleeping too?

## WHY DO DOGS WALK IN CIRCLES BEFORE LYING DOWN?

Another main theory is the before-mentioned keen sense of smell a dog possesses. We lock our doors at night. A dog spreads its scent out in a big area as a sort of force field by circling around and lying down in the middle of the area.

Obscure fact: Humans sleep an average of 8 out of 24 hours. Dogs sleep an average of 18 out of 24 hours.

## WHY IS NEW YEAR'S DAY CELEBRATED ON JANUARY 1ST?

In the long history of man, only in the last 400 years has January 1st been the widely accepted start of the New Year. Before that, New Year's Day could fall anywhere from the old British March 25th to Easter Sunday. The Italians in the Middle Ages used December 15th which must have wreaked havoc with department store Santas having to hear both Christmas wishes and New Year's Resolutions at the same time!

Originally, the calendar was puppet to political whim, falling prey to big shots wanting longer terms in office. The New Year was routinely celebrated as the beginning of Spring—on March 25th. The Roman senate in 153 B.C. declared January 1st as the start of the year because public festival dates were in such confusion.

Obscure fact: Julius Caesar in 46 B.C. let the year plod on for 445 days to reset the calendar to January 1st, earning the notation of the Julian Calendar and a pat on the back by Brutus.

Being a native New Mexican, a Christmas is not a Christmas without the softly glowing candles in small paper bags lining the driveway, sidewalk, and any other flat surface. The tradition stems from the Mexican/Hispanic influence that makes the Southwest so culturally rich. Simply put, the tradition is symbolic of lighting a pathway for the Christ child.

## WHAT WAS THE GREAT LUMINARIO DEBATE?

Here's the problem: All my life, we called the little bags with sand holding candles luminarios. Then as suddenly as Haley's comet became Haley's comet, purists were telling us we were all wrong. They should be called *farilitos* (or little fires). Luminarios, they now say, are the little bonfires lit on Christmas Eve.

From now on, I'm calling them bagalitos!

## WHY DOES EASTER FALL ON DIFFERENT DAYS?

*The College of Obscure Knowledge*

Like nearly all of our holidays, Easter was originally a pagan celebration—the annual start of Spring celebrating the Anglo-Saxon goddess Eastre (or Eostre). Early missionaries seized on the opportunity to turn it into a holiday, much like the origin of Christmas, turning the rite of Spring into the observation of the Resurrection of Jesus.

Originally, Easter was celebrated on Jewish Passover, which could fall on any day of the week. Early Church fathers wanted the celebration of the Resurrection celebrated on a Sunday. So, the Emperor Constantine convened the Council of Nicaea, and they sent out the decree which is followed to this day: Easter will be celebrated on the first Sunday after the first full moon on or after the vernal equinox. The vernal equinox is March 21st of each year, so we could have Easter anytime between March 22nd and April 25th.

Thank goodness we don't have to figure it out since it's on the calendar every year!

69

We thought we'd find a town named Smithereens on the map, but alas, no.

Common belief must be that smithereens is a state of disassembly, to be politically correct. Actually, *smithers* comes from the Irish *smidirin* meaning "a small piece of the whole—a fragment or a particle." The same place we get the word *smidgen* from.

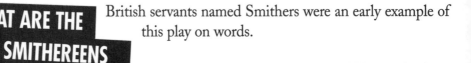

**WHAT ARE THE SMITHEREENS THAT YOU CAN GET BLOWN TO?**

British servants named Smithers were an early example of this play on words.

*Smithereens* is a fun word that should be put back into common usage. Not much, just a smithereen. Think of the TV jingles: "Brylcream, a little smithereen will do ya. . . ."

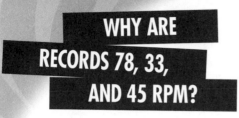

# WHY ARE RECORDS 78, 33, AND 45 RPM?

Records? Oh . . . those big flat vinyl things. I remember those!

The history of recorded music is a classic story of industry versus technology. The first record players were hand-cranked, so you had a choice between making ice cream or listening to music. Hand cranking was about 80 revolutions per minute (RPM's). When the electric motor was installed, they ran at 78.26, and that was close enough. Problem was, 78's booked through music in about 5 minutes. 33 ⅓ records, however, offered longer playing time (LP) at great fidelity.

Here came the corporations. RCA tried to introduce the 33 ⅓ in 1931. Timing and marketing combined to make that a disaster. Columbia, with their new microgroove system introduced the 33 ⅓ successfully in 1948, and even offered the process gratis to any company that would use it as a standard. RCA countered with the 45. In the 50's, both albums and singles were made by all.

Then came CD's. Playing at a constant 300 RPM with laser light decoding digital information, it has made vinyl all but obsolete.

71

We have often compared broadcasting to soap operas—you have a job for two or three years and then move on. You get to know those who stay in one place for awhile. The rest are an endless parade of new faces.

The main reason is that news reporters and disc jockeys make a pitiful salary, and they are all looking to move up either to that anchorman's job, or in radio, that morning show or management job. Most are in a stair-step position using your current town as a steppingstone to a bigger town. Station management really frowns on making a big announcement to say someone has just snagged a better job.

## WHY DO DJ'S AND NEWS REPORTERS DISAPPEAR WITHOUT A WORD?

Obscure fact: Due to the Telecommunications Act of 1996, local radio station ownership will be a rarity as large corporations gobble up all the stations and merge staffs, costing thousands of jobs.

# WHO DECIDES WHOSE FACE GOES ON OUR MONEY?

The Secretary of the Treasury decides what great American will grace our coins and bills, as decreed by an act of Congress in 1962. Most of our current money mugs were selected in 1928 after several years of meetings and a committee formed by then Secretary of the Treasury, Andrew Mellon. Only presidents were to be featured, but Mellon felt Alexander Hamilton and Ben Franklin were revered enough to be enshrined on currency.

Obscure (this is not a joke) fact: Martha Washington was once on a bill—one of the first-ever-issued Silver Certificates.

Obscure goofup fact: A star or asterisk instead of a letter in front of a serial number on a bill means that the bill is a substitute for one that was thrown out due to a printing imperfection.

Wasn't this on an episode of "All in the Family?"

This question has always bothered me. When I went on the radio with it, I found some interesting facts. Half of the population of the United States demands their toilet paper to be positioned one particular way; the other half could care less. An impromptu survey came up with no answer on the tissue issue, so we called the two major hotels in Tulsa, Oklahoma: the Adams Mark and the DoubleTree, asked for housekeeping, and BOTH hotels say the standard is over the top. Not satisfied, we called the Waldolf Astoria in New York to help in this swirling controversy, and they say over the top.

Obscure fact: Hotels fold the end of the roll to show you that housekeeping has been there and that you will be the first to use it after cleaning.

**WHAT IS REALLY CORRECT FOR T-PAPER? OVER OR UNDER?**

## WHY DO SO MANY ELDERLY PEOPLE EAT AT CAFETERIAS?

To my delight and surprise, extensive research has already been done on this by one of my heroes, David Feldman, in the first of his *Imponderables* books. Some of the highlights he mentions are cafeterias are located where older folks live, seniors dine out slightly more than the average, price, portion size, home cooking, and the fact that seniors like to linger longer and cafeterias don't rush them out the door.

Having the distinct advantage of a wife who is Resident Services Director of a world-renowned retirement village, and the distinct pleasure of a retirement-age mom who we dine out with weekly, I have been informed the main reason is independence—for the same reason seniors would rather drive than fly. They hate to hand over control—especially to a wait staff. They like to see the food they are getting—no surprises. The seniors we know hate to have plates taken and to feel rushed. The main reason they like eating out in cafeterias is that they know the price and don't have to wait for their bill.

Some theorize just because of the caffeine.

Others say because adults always seemed to like it, so we made ourselves like it too.

No one really knows why we like this hot, bitter beverage, though coffee experts say it is due to the complex flavors that only a roasted substance can possess. (If that's true, give me a T-bone!) Believe it or not, the answer is close to that. Experts tell us there are 400 chemical composites that blend into the flavor, and many say the warmth, aroma, and acquired taste is akin to meat.

## WHY DO WE LIKE COFFEE ANYWAY?

Obscure historical facts: No one can agree on the origin of coffee, though it can definitely be traced back to Arab origins in the 9th or 10th centuries A.D. Some credit an Arabian doctor named Rhazes. Others name him Avicenna.

Another version is of a shepherd boy who found his goats frolicking as high as a kite after an espresso meal and had a vision to boil the beans into a drink.

## WHAT IS SASPARILLA, AND CAN WE BUY IT NOWADAYS?

You're saying, "I know this one! Root Beer!!" Buzzzzzz. Wrong. Sasparilla is actually a vine found in the tropics complete with Tarzan's palm prints.

Now, forget that fact because the vine sasparilla has nothing to do with the drink. Old west sasparilla was a blend of oils: birch, anise, ginger, and a squeeze of lemon oil mixed with sassafras tree root (hence, root beer).

Sassafras was a common home remedy in the 1800's, and any drink made out of it was thought to have healing properties. That sassafras-parilla concoction did taste a bit like our modern-day root beer, without all the sugar and any carbonation. Yum.

Obscure fact: Root beer is created from desert yucca sap which Native Americans used as soap. Yum.

There are!
You have one if you are a cat owner.

Domestic cats are the miniatures compared to the wild big cats, and we have bred them about as small as they can go. On the other paw, there are no big dogs in the wild. In fact, hyenas, wolves, and coyotes are small compared to our larger domestic dog breeds. One of my sources goes into detail about genetic engineering of cats compared to dogs, and simply translated it just means a cat's genetic makeup is not as flexible as a dog's.

## WHY ARE THERE MINIATURE DOGS, BUT NO MINIATURE CATS?

Obscure possible fact: After doing this topic on the air, a listener called to say there is now a new breed of miniature cats called Munchkin Cats. I have tried to confirm this, and cannot tell you for sure if I am on the short end of a . . . um . . . tall "tail."

## WHY DO DOGS JERK THEIR HIND LEGS WHEN YOU SCRATCH THEIR TUMMIES?

Mainly to amuse their owners.

There are several examples of similar, unexplained phenomena in humans: an itch that wanders all over your back, hunger pains from aromas, laughing when tickled, a shudder from hearing chalk on a blackboard, and that ache you get when someone describes their operation.

Experts say dogs are just wired up that way, much like a doctor tapping your knee will make it bounce. Others fall back to instinct controlling your pet's line of thinking which has your dog's hind legs doing everything from fending off predators, to flicking away parasites, to thinking it's drowning and wanting to dog paddle.

Here in the Marble's household we have two dogs (one just for emergencies). One dog will do the hind-end shuffle like a drummer playing "Wipe Out" while the other just isn't ticklish at all.

**The College of Obscure Knowledge**

The old man is a reoccurring symbol throughout mankind—either portraying wisdom and fortitude, or just plain ready to retire the year, put on blue double-knit pants, and head the RV down to Florida.

The baby is a very familiar symbol of hope and renewal all through history, even to the point of widespread child sacrifice by the ancients. Egyptian, Greek, and Roman use of the symbol of a child for New Year's was so ingrained into celebrations that the Early Church made sure it was the Christ child, and not a pagan symbol that was portrayed.

## WHY ARE THE SYMBOLS FOR NEW YEAR'S AN OLD MAN AND A BABY?

By modern times, the religious significance of the symbolism was gone. German immigrants to America brought with them our current incarnation of the diapered baby holding a banner printed with the new year.

(You know—the new year we must remember to write on our checks!).

## WAS THERE A REAL ST. VALENTINE?

Yes! The real story, however, is shrouded by lore and legend, as with other dashing, heroic, romantic, historical figures.

One legend has Valentine as a Bishop of Terni, Italy—a rescuer of children imprisoned for not worshiping Roman gods. The prevailing story has our Valentine in Rome at odds with the Emperor Claudius about 270 A.D. Claudius had abolished marriage so soldiers wouldn't have family ties in attempts to make them braver in battle. Bishop Valentine performed marriages in secret until he was caught, clubbed, and beheaded on February 14th. Some stories say Valentine, while awaiting execution, during his last weeks, taught lessons to the blind daughter of the jailer.

He described the world of nature to Julia, taught her arithmetic, shared stories about God and about how to pray.

During this time Julia's sight was miraculously restored. On the eve of his death, Valentinus wrote a farewell note to Julia signed "From Your Valentine." It is said that Julia planted an almond tree near his grave, which still lives today as a symbol of abiding love and friendship. This is believed to be the foundation for exchanging messages of affection, love, and devotion—a tradition shared around the world to this day.

81

The College of Obscure Knowledge Back in the mid 1980's, during our time of service to Q106 in Santa Fe/Albuquerque, our guest co-host one day was then-governor of New Mexico, Gary Carruthers. We thumbed through a trivia book and found a governmental, yet unpolitical type quiz question: what does *e pluribus unim* mean (as found on the Great Seal of the United States)?

According to the trivia book, we awarded the prize (a t-shirt or a taco or something) to the caller who responded that it means "In God We Trust." Wrong.

## WHAT DOES E PLURIBUS UNIM MEAN?

*E Pluribus Unim* is the Latin phrase translated "from many, one." You can imagine the howls from the intelligentsia who got it right, were told otherwise, and wanted their tacos. We found ourselves written up in print in the local newspapers, and the answer seared into our memory.

Obscure translations: The reverse side of the Great Seal, also on our dollar bill *Annuit copetis* translates "God has favored our undertaking." *Novus ordo Seclorum* translates "new order of the ages." (Or at least that's what is in print.)

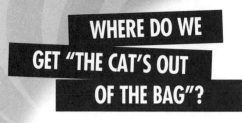

## WHERE DO WE GET "THE CAT'S OUT OF THE BAG"?

Meaning a secret is revealed, images of kittens playing with a grocery sack come to mind. Nope.

First of all, remember that bags as we know them, are a very recent invention. When you hear any old saying that mentions bag (or the old poke), you're talking burlap sacks. There were no cardboard boxes, no paper, no plastic. Everything was carried in bags made of cloth, burlap, or skins.

Shopping was quite different, too. There were no grocery stores. There were open-air markets or goods straight from the farm. So, you could carry your dinner home wriggling in your hands or in a bag (perhaps the first Piggly Wiggly?).

This is also where the phrase *pig in a poke* comes from. Unscrupulous sellers would substitute a worthless (and plentiful) cat in place of the piglet without the buyer finding out until (say it all together) the cat was out of the bag. Evidently this practice was so common, it found its way into common slang.

Like my colleague Seth Andrews says, "It's like taking a painting to a museum and asking them to display it for you."

Every radio station receives tons of prospective ads a week. Record company representatives call every week to see what song has been added, and to push a particular song or artist.

I'll let you in on a couple of secrets: Secret one. Record companies push certain artists, and certain songs have a bounty on them. If this song is added to the play list of a station, the record rep gets a bonus. The bigger the market (or city) the bigger the bonus.

## WHY DOESN'T THE RADIO STATION PLAY MY DEMO TAPE?

Secret two. Most stations don't have the personnel to listen to, review, and format test each song (or don't trust someone to do it right), so they hire a consultant to do it for them.

To get back to the question, unless you are signed with a major record label, and they are pushing to make you a star, it's pretty unlikely any station will play your song.

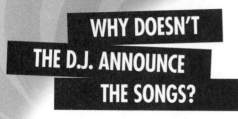
## WHY DOESN'T THE D.J. ANNOUNCE THE SONGS?

We are not being lazy!

We are doing what we are told. Yes, that same paranoia about ratings and listeners has not only affected format and music, but your announcers as well. With few exceptions, radio stations in competitive situations tell their D.J.'s what to say, and when to say it. Serious. If they don't tell you who sang that song, it's because they were told not to at that particular break or time.

Why? Management hires a guy from out of town and relies on this consultant's advice on every detail of what you hear. Chances are, the content, length, and even speed of delivery are carefully monitored. Believe it or not, that carefree announcer is scrutinized on every word when he gets off the air in a torturous ceremony called an air check.

And people still ask me if I miss high-pressure commercial radio!

85

They are in a ratings period.

Imagine this: in your business, an outside company comes in and asks your customers questions about you and your competitors, then compiles a book of ratings based on a survey of 2-3 percent of the population. Then, that book of ratings determines your revenue for the next few months. Now you get an idea of what broadcasters go through. Broadcasters will do anything to get those ratings, because without them, it means financial death.

## WHY DOES EVERY RADIO STATION HAVE CONTESTS AT THE SAME TIME?

Anymore, cities of any size are constantly in rating periods of radio. But watch for increased advertising and contesting by radio stations in the Fall and Spring, coinciding with when advertisers plan their ad buys when the rating results come out.

## HOW DID THEY LOCK SALOON DOORS IN THE OLD WEST?

You would think that those swinging doors would be as ineffective in slowing down someone as a locked bathroom stall would slow down a kid who really needed to go.

Hate to pop yet another myth of the Old West, but those swinging doors are a Hollywood invention. Some real fancy places had similar doors, beads, or curtains separating an entryway from the saloon itself. Those were purely decorative with real, solid, locking doors sharing the same frame, but rarely were the swinging doors facing the street. Then came Hollywood: it just didn't look the same with John Wayne tossing someone through the doors out into the foyer.

Obscure fact: Before electricity, saloons, eating establishments, and homes in the Old West kept drinks and perishables cool either in a cistern or a root cellar.

87

To make it easier for your servants to dress you.

Buttons stem from the 1300's and French aristocracy. (Before that, we assume everything was fastened by Velcro.) With right-handed people being the majority, it is easiest to push a button with your right hand through a hole held by the left. All of my sources say this is where the arrangement was reversed to help the handmaidens dress the rich. Rich guys evidently dressed themselves (but like today, still couldn't find their socks).

## WHY DO MEN'S AND WOMEN'S SHIRTS BUTTON FROM DIFFERENT DIRECTIONS?

Here's a couple of other interesting theories; right-handed men needed an easy way to keep hands warm (a la Napoleon), and when drawing your sword (right hand to left hip), you didn't want to catch a lapel.

Obscure fact: In a recent Civil War battlefield excavation there were lots of little white buttons mixed in with the bones—a mystery solved when an old-timer identified them as underwear buttons.

# WHAT IS A SARDINE, REALLY?

Are you ready for this? There is no such thing as a sardine. You can't fish for it, and you can't buy it in a market. It's like hunting for a Spam animal.

Sardine is just a nickname for any kind of small fish that comes packaged in a flat can. So what are sardine eaters eating? There are over 20 possibilities—that's how many different species of fish could be in there laughing their heads off. In North America, most sardines are small herring. Around the world, different countries prefer other things like anchovies and pilchards. I am not a fan particularly, but I am told each tastes the same due to the similar processing, though texture varies.

Obscure facts: Sardines were popular as a low-cost protein meal in the early part of this century, peaking in the Depression years. Too much was fed to our boys during the war, sales dropped after World War II, and sales still stink.

It is a breed of particularly small fowl, raised exclusively in Cornwall for the amusement of the Royal Family; Prince Charles is said to have bagged 30 of them in a record hunt. (The preceding statement is pure fabrication. I was just seeing how gullible you are.)

Cornish game hen is to chicken what veal is to beef. It's one of those secrets they keep from you while young, and by the time you find out, you're past

**WHAT IS A CORNISH GAME HEN?**

caring. Most Cornish game hens are plain old young chickens, less than a month old and less than a pound. In fact, federal guidelines say the bird must be under two pounds to be classified as a Cornish game hen. So, like a barnyard version of *Logan's Run*, chicken littles are in a race against time and weight. Once past that point, you are guaranteed a few more years until the Colonel comes knocking.

## WHAT IS THE DIFFERENCE BETWEEN A PIG AND A HOG?

Oh, that's easy. I have been called both. It just depends on the situation. A pig is when you eat way too much, and a hog is when you eat so much that others don't get their share.

Oh, you mean the animals! In England, there is no difference between a hog and a pig. Swine are swine. Here in the colonies, you are a pig until you weigh over 180 pounds, then you are officially a hog.

Obscure fact: Pigs are the only animal besides man that can actually get a sunburn.

Linguistic obscure fact: A grouping is called a sounder of swine.

Worthless obscure fact: The biggest hog ever recorded was in 1939 in North Carolina. He was named Big Boy, tipping the scales at 1,904 pounds.

Mainly because this breed of dog loves horses. In fact, their nickname is coach dogs.

Dalmatia is in Croatia in the western part of what's left of the troubled Yugoslavia. This is where Dalmatians originated and were bred as watch dogs. When their affinity for horses became apparent, they were used for everything from training, to shepherding, to hunting, to draft dogs alongside mounted soldiers.

## WHY ARE DALMATIANS ASSOCIATED WITH FIRE HOUSES?

In early America, everything was done by horse. You can just imagine the fire houses back then—not the large garages with shiny engines we have now, but they were more or less stables ready to pull a fire wagon. Dalmatians became a familiar sight, running beside the wagon, or running ahead of the horses clearing a way. When them new-fangled gasoline machines came along, the need of the dog diminished, except for using them as mascots.

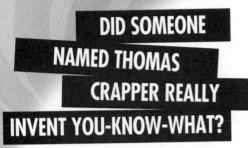

## DID SOMEONE NAMED THOMAS CRAPPER REALLY INVENT YOU-KNOW-WHAT?

No. The first flush toilet was on the island of Crete 4,000 years ago. For some reason, invention in this direction regressed to chamber pots until an Englishman named Alexander Cumming invented our modern fixture with the odor-blocking sink trap in 1775.

The controversy centers around a man named Thomas Crapper. Did he exist? There is evidence that he existed and may have improved on the invention. Many say Tom and his name are just a hoax of one Wallace Reyburn who in 1969 published *Flushed with Pride: The Story of Thomas Crapper*. No kidding.

Obscure fact: The word *toilet* comes from the French word for a cloth covering a dressing table, then later to the objects on the dressing table (as in toilet water), and only in America does it refer to the porcelain appliance.

Even more obscure fact: Henry Wadsworth Longfellow in 1840 was the first American to have plumbing installed in his home.

93

Yes! We know some facts about him, but the rest is steeped in Irish folklore. We do know he was not Irish.

He was born about 385 A.D., most likely in Wales. His village was overrun, and he was sold into slavery at age 16. Escaping that, he spent at least a dozen years in Gaul at a monastery studying under St. Germain, after which he returned to Ireland and 30 fruitful years of turning Druids into Christians. He died March 17th, 461 A.D.

## WAS THERE A REAL ST. PATRICK?

Now the fun stuff. Lore and legend surround Patrick, the most famous being a sermon he delivered that scared the snakes out of everybody. He is also credited with making snow into fire and raising the dead.

Obscure fact: Patrick is said to have used the three-leafed shamrock as a symbol of the Trinity, hence the association with the holiday.

# WHY ARE U.S. ELECTIONS HELD ON TUESDAYS?

*The College of Obscure Knowledge*

The truth? Because it sometimes takes days to ride to the polling places, and then, when the votes are hand-counted by lantern light, it takes days to ride throughout the state informing the barely literate populous of the decision. That's the truth.

In 1845, Congress decreed the National Election Day, timing it so the Electoral College would have 34 days or so to finally get the news about the election results. The Tuesday following the first Monday in November was chosen. Why not Monday? The ride to the polls might involve taboo travel during Sunday. Why not the first Tuesday? It might fall on the first of the month and would cause all sorts of business problems (not to mention long buggy lines at the ATM).

A horse's teeth tell its age in several ways and give rise to several common sayings, such as; "don't look a gift horse in the mouth," and "straight from the horses mouth."

Here's the scoop! At 2 years, the first permanent teeth in the center of the lower jaw come in. One year later, a second pair come in beside them, and a third pair emerge after the horse is 4 years old. If you know what to look for, you can get pretty close to the age.

## WHY DO WE SAY "LONG IN THE TOOTH"?

Then, they say a horse's gums recede in old age. Use your horse sense to figure out why we say "long in the tooth by gum."

Obscure fact: Did you know, contrary to what they teach us on TV, that horses cannot talk?

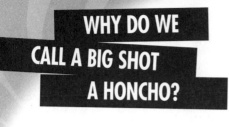

## WHY DO WE CALL A BIG SHOT A HONCHO?

The College of Obscure Knowledge

Being raised in the Southwest, we always thought this was Spanish in origin. You know—honcho, pancho, taco, burrito. Wrongorito.

The word is Japanese in origin!

We use it as slang for someone in charge or with power. The original meaning was a term of respect for the head of a squad. Honcho is akin to sarge. A similar word is tycoon, from the Japanese *taikun*, more familiar to us as shogun.

Obscure notion: An unreliable source tells us the word *Sushi* comes from the original word for stomach parasites.

Second verse, same as the first. They are in a ratings period.

The networks roll out the new shows in November, do those cliffhangers in May, and focus mid-season in February because those are ratings months. So is July, but it's not regarded as important as the other three sweeps months.

Local TV stations rely on their local news to determine ratings, and some even go the radio-ratings route and do contests. I hosted a one-minute game show in the 80's called "Spin to Win" where the secret word was given out during the newscast.

**WHY DOES TV NEWS SEEM TO BE MORE SENSATIONAL AT TIMES?**

Most TV stations use the sweeps to overwork their reporters to do special reports with the hope you will be glued to the tube and name them in the ratings.

## WHAT ARE THOSE BEEPS I HEAR ON THE RADIO?

Those beeps are signals to tell someone that it's time to do something.

There are various types of beeps. These include the high-tech beep—a multi-tone signal to alert computers and machines to change from one network, satellite, or channel to another. A dual-tone signal—such as the EBS tone that trips or starts a machine. Single tones, many of which you cannot hear, such as tones on the end of commercials—which start the next commercial in a machine. Tones inaudible to humans found on one standard piece of audio equipment called the cart machine, start and stop recordings. Tones are sent via satellite—to start local equipment at precise times.

Low tech tones like the ones the networks air to wake up D.J.'s before newscasts, and in pre-taped programs—tones used as a countdown more or less. Not really necessary, but they sound neat.

You've heard the phrase, "If you don't use it, you'll lose it." They were talking about voices. Few people ever learn how to use their voice correctly!

Basic biology of voice; you run controlled air over vocal cords. The best way to breathe that controlled air is gut level using the diaphragm, avoiding the nasal passages. Some great voices are born, but the majority of great voices are made after years of coaching.

Not counting tissue shrinkage, or tumor-inducing wavers, aging voices are caused by lack of respiratory dynamics—not enough air forced through the vocal cords because they never learned how. Other voices get lazy with nasal tones (young whippersnappers!) when the breathing becomes more difficult. On trained voices, like aging actors, singers, or radio announcers, little difference is discernable.

**WHY DO OUR VOICES SOUND DIFFERENT AS WE AGE?**

Obscure fact: Walter Brennan's much imitated cougar-like voice came from getting a lung-full of mustard gas in World War I.

## WAS EGGS BENEDICT NAMED AFTER THE TRAITOR?

No. But that's about all my sources can agree upon.

There are no less than three people named Benedict who are credited with the dish consisting of poached eggs on ham on toast (preferable an English muffin) covered with Hollandaise.

First of all, there is a St. Benedict. The dish is said not only to be created by him, but named in his honor.

Then there is the turn-of-the-century banker E.C. Benedict who is said to have served this on his yacht where he entertained yachts of guests.

My favorite story is that a wealthy New Yorker named Sam Benedict, who the legend says would order this at the Waldorf-Astoria as a breakfast hangover remedy after a night on the town. The chef at the hotel named the dish in his dubious honor.

Driving down the highway, seeing a cider stand, stopping, and taking home a jug has to be one of life's simple pleasures—the assumption always being that cider is a homemade, tangy, barely-legal concoction made from squeezin's and dripped out of pappy's still.

Turns out we were raised on the right, if not totally correct idea. It's all in the processing.

## WHAT'S THE DIFFERENCE BETWEEN CIDER AND JUICE?

Juice is flavor squeezed from just about anything, filtered and pasteurized, usually sweetened beyond belief, and sold to markets.

Cider retains a sharp or tangy taste without all the processing (apple cider aficionados prefer first-season tart apples) and without all the added sweetening. Be warned though! Cider will ferment over time. Maybe that's where I got my pappy's still image from.

## WHY DON'T BIRDS TIP OVER WHEN THEY SLEEP ON A WIRE?

They don't weigh much, and they have a perfect sense of balance. Plus a couple of other things you might not realize:

A bird's claws are like nature's perfect vice-grips. It takes little more than its own body weight to work them. The tendons in the toes, activated by body weight, perform the locking maneuver.

The second part of the bird's anti-tip mechanism is tiny spike-like ratchets on the underside of its claw. They feel rough, like a cat's tongue when touched. Microscopically, they lock in and hold a bird upright when asleep.

Obscure fact: Why don't birds fry on electric wires? One wire won't do it. Now if a bird or squirrel or Wichita lineman touches one hot wire and a ground—or two wires are touched simultaneously— viola! Flambe!

*The College of Obscure Knowledge* Ah yes, that tranquil fall ritual of seeing swarms of flies migrating south in that familiar V formation. . . .

No, they don't migrate. They all die off in the winter. Well, not all.

Flies are much like humans in temperature tolerance. They can't get too hot or humid, and they'll die if it's freezing. But a fly's life span is short—20 days max. It can live longer in the larval or pupal stage (my pupal stage was about 12 years until I graduated), but not a whole winter. Some survive in man-made structures, others underground.

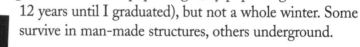

**DO FLIES MIGRATE IN THE WINTER?**

Obscure fact: Always at least 2 flies at a time survive through several generations throughout the winter months until it's party time. Then it is estimated that a single pair of flies can produce, in one summer, over three trillion little tax deductions.

# WHY DO WE ASSOCIATE BUNNIES AND EGGS WITH EASTER?

Bunnies: The hare has been there from the beginning. The original celebration of Easter, that pagan rite of Spring, was symbolized by the hare as a fertility symbol.

Eggs: Eggs were another spring-like fertility symbol associated with the holiday, but have been given as gifts from the beginning of time. Egyptians put them atop tombs. Greeks put them atop graves. I put them atop enchiladas. In the 1800's eggs-uberance reached its peak with the goldsmith Peter Carl Faberge handcrafting priceless works of art encased in the shape of an egg, the most famous one being commissioned by Czar Alexander the Third as a gift to his wife.

Possible obscure fact: Currently in the western world, one cannot think of Easter eggs without thinking of the clucking of the Cadbury candy egg.

**The College of Obscure Knowledge**

For the same reason we eat hot dogs on Labor Day. They're on sale!

Easter, originally a pagan Spring festival turned into a holy day, was originally celebrated on Jewish Passover. When early villagers turned into Christian converts, they didn't need much of an excuse to put an apple in a pig's mouth and dig a BBQ pit at any old time, no matter what the holiday. The English started eating bacon during the holiday as a symbol of freedom from the Mosaic Law's prohibition of pork, perhaps in defiance of the Jewish holiday.

## WHY DO WE EAT HAM AT EASTER?

It is said that in the eleventh century that William the Conqueror preferred ham over bacon, so he decreed a switch. The rest is history.

Obscure fact: Lamb is preferred in Mediterranean and European cultures on Easter.

## WHY DO WE USE RX FOR A PRESCRIPTION?

This sounds far-fetched, but it is documented.

Rx is from the Latin term *recepta* which means "take." A form of the same word is *recipere* which means "acquire." (So we have our give and take.) If these words look familiar, we get the words *receive*, *receipt*, and *recipe* from this same source. Originally, Rx was a list of ingredients—a recipe of any kind. Over time, the term became associated exclusively with medicine.

Obscure consumer alert: Have you noticed all the direct to consumer advertising of prescription-only drugs recently? That kind of advertising has been legal since 1985, but only since the proliferation of HMO's, or managed care, where doctors are limited in the drugs they can prescribe, are we seeing the drug companies hoping you will pressure your provider into using their products.

Here is another example of a phrase so common that every single book of literary clichés has it. Yet, none have come up with the same story twice! Here are some theories:

To beat around the bush is an obvious reference to some early hunting practice, and many sources have left it at that. Several said nets were put over a bush full of birds, and kids would raise a racket to fill the net full of escaping birds.

**WHY DO WE SAY "BEAT AROUND THE BUSH"?**

One source said the phrase came from boar hunting with unarmed beaters circumventing the dangerous creatures, yet scaring the beasts towards the hunters. Charles Earle Funk relates the ancient sport of batfowling which is described as something like Babe Ruth on a skeet range. Hunters would venture out at night, someone would scare the birds to take flight, hopefully towards the light, and the guys would club them in midair.

Obscure thought: Perhaps this is where the baseball term *"fowl"* came from!

## WAS THERE EVER A MR. KODAK?

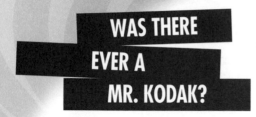

With the name of the company being Eastman Kodak, there had to be, right? Wrong!

According to the *New York Library Book of Answers*, the name is the brainchild of George Eastman, who said, "I knew a trade name must be short, vigorous, incapable of being misspelled . . . and in order to satisfy trademark laws, it must mean nothing. The letter K had been a favorite with me, it seemed a strong, incisive sort of letter. Then it became a question of trying out a great number of combinations of letters that made words starting and ending with K. Not to be confused with the bear that has one more letter and syllable (or the Telly Savalas TV character), the word *Kodak* was born.

Obscure fact: Mesa Verde National Park has an Anazasi Cliff Dwelling Ruin named Kodak House (most likely because early explorers stored film there).

109

No. Sanka is a conglomeration of the French phrase *sans cafeine* which translated means, "why bother. . . ."

The process of taking the caffeine out of coffee beans was discovered by accident in 1903. The story goes that an American coffee importer ordered a shipload of coffee from Europe, and on the way, saltwater leaked into the hold, soaking the cargo. To everyone's surprise, the flavor and quality of the beans remained intact, but the caffeine had naturally washed away into the sea. By no coincidence, we understand sharks were docile vegetarians until 1903.

**WAS THERE EVER A MR. SANKA?**

Obscure fact: Decaf carafes in restaurants usually have orange or green handles as identification due to the popularity of the brand Sanka.

# HOW COME ICE CUBES ARE SOMETIMES CLEAR, SOMETIMES CLOUDY?

Tiny bubbles... not the song, but the facts.

Ever watch tap water coming out of the tap? (Next to watching grass grow, one of my favorite pastimes.) Chances are, water from your faucet is forced through an aerator, making that pleasant full-stream flow, and putting air in your water.

Sometimes a glass of water will look cloudy, then slowly clear up. That is exactly what happens in your freezer. If your freezer is super-cold and freezes things quickly, those tiny bubbles stay in a cloudy cube.

Inversely, if your freezer is slow to form cubes, the bubbles have time to pack, tidy up, call a mover, and leave town, leaving clear cubes.

Obscure fact: Home automatic ice makers make crescent-shaped ice so the cubes will drop out. That's the shape of ice which is least likely to stick.

It depends on where you eat your steak!

Keep this in mind if ever you buy a half of beef. Only a very small part of the cow has the really good steaks. That's why steak is so expensive. You've got your ribs, your prime ribs, then the sirloin. These areas are highly marbled—full of fat—and, therefore, more tender and tasty.

Legend has it that royalty in ages past when there wasn't a Sizzler or Bonanza anywhere, loved a particular steak so much that he knighted it sir-loin! Cute, but wrong. Sirloin is actually from the French *surlonge* meaning "just above the loin".

## WHAT'S THE DIFFERENCE BETWEEN SIRLOIN, K.C., OR NEW YORK STEAK?

In answer to the question, there is no difference between a New York or a Kansas City sirloin. It's a marketing tool to make you feel proud of where the cow came from!

Obscure fact: The Porter House in New York made the big slab-o-T-bone famous.

112

## WHAT ARE THE SAFEST DOGS?

The toothless ones?
Again, we turn to a study in
New York.

Dogs That Bite the Least are the
Golden Retriever, Labrador Retriever, Shetland Sheepdog, Old English Sheepdog, and the Welsh Terrier.

(We assume from this list that the statisticians were from Great Britain and just claimed to be from New York.)

Note of Caution: Recent reports say high-volume for profit puppy farms are now inadvertently breeding away some of the gentleness of popular breeds like the retrievers.

Obscure tragic fact: Three thousand puppies are born every second. Nearly 200,000 puppies were born since you started reading this page! Very few will find homes.

Earnest request: Please spay or neuter your pup!

You can take the lion out of the jungle, but you can't take the jungle out of the lion.

You have your predator and you have your prey. Lions are predators. No amount of domestication will change that or make caged animals predictable. We all are familiar with the tragedies when an elephant or other animal goes berserk.

Here is the secret lion tamers know. You can tell when a lion is going to strike! Lions are lazy by nature, but if hungry, threatened, or ticked off, a lion will pounce. Lion tamers know the individual animal, know its limits, and watch for the telltale signs; not growling, not swatting paws, but eyes narrowed and ears back.

## WHY DO LION TAMERS USE CHAIRS?

If this happens, instant distraction is called for, such as whips, guns, etc. As anyone who has watched "Wild Kingdom" or nature films knows, a lion in the midst of stalking his prey is the picture of ultimate concentration. A chair in the face breaks that concentration to pieces—four points of distraction to be precise (five if using an office chair!).

# WHAT IS THE ORIGIN OF MOTHER'S DAY?

It was a one-woman crusade of West Virginian Anna Jarvis that brought the day to reality around 1907.

Three years after her mother's death, Anna Jarvis organized the Mother's Day International Association. It resulted in a presidential proclamation by Woodrow Wilson in 1914. Carnations were her mother's favorite flower. Jarvis came up with the idea of a red carnation for a living mother, a white carnation as a tribute to a mother already passed on.

In case Mom is reading and wants to correct me, the singular possessive—Mother's Day—is correct by executive decree, not Mothers Day, as some would have it.

Two obscure facts: Jarvis reportedly regretted the action and hated the commercialization of the holiday, including Mother's Day cards. And by the way, Jarvis never became a mother herself!

115

We use it today in the same way we use "getting down to business" or "getting to the core of the matter." The origin? You decide! Every literary source has a different story, and each one claims to be the truth. Here are some of the theories we found:

Many claim the basis for this phrase is Old English cloth shops. Supposedly they had brass tacks nailed to the counter to assist in buying fabric by the yard. Charles Earle Funk says that supposition is wrong, that the term came from a modern practice of using tacks of modern manufacture. He suggests the saying is nautical, meaning "to scrape barnacles off a ship until you expose the copper bolts or brass tacks."

## WHAT DOES "GETTING DOWN TO BRASS TACKS" MEAN?

Yet another source says brass is an Old English nickname for money. (We wonder why anything authors are not quite sure of must be of Old English origin.)

Obscure notion: A political fan of the College suggests brass tacks must be revenue enhancement for trumpet players. (Say it out loud, and you'll get it.)

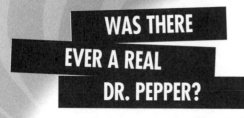

## WAS THERE
## EVER A REAL
## DR. PEPPER?

The College of Obscure Knowledge

Yes. It's a story of unrequited love at the hands of a heartless Dr. Pepper!

Back in the 1800's in Rural Retreat, Virginia, there was a sure-enough Dr. Pepper. (One of my sources says his name was Kenneth. One says it was Charles.) The good Dr. hired a young pharmacist named Wade Morrison, to work in his drug store. A romance developed between Morrison and Dr. Pepper's daughter. The Dr. thought Morrison too old and sent him packing. He wound up in Waco, Texas, starting his own corner drug store. One of his pharmacists/soda jerks concocted the fruity soft drink. Evidently, the town folk knew about the story and suggested the name. The year is thought to be 1885, making it the oldest major soft drink in America.

Obscure fact #1: Despite rumor, there is no prune juice in Dr. Pepper.

Obscure fact #2: There is a Dr. Pepper Museum in Waco where about 100 people a day visit.

Obscure fact #3: The "10, 2, and 4" on the bottles signified the perfect in-between meal times to revitalize with a swig of Dr. Pepper.

Because mattresses are getting thicker. No joke!

In post World War II America, when tract homes and cookie-cutter subdivisions became the norm, the mattress companies started marketing the fact that you spend a third of your life in bed and that your life would be much better with some sleep.

In the 1960's, suburbia discovered what those of us raised in the wild know as fact; the firmer the mattress the better your back. This concept stated a round of "innerspring" this and "magic-coil" that. Gradually, mattresses started getting thicker and thicker . . . from a once standard 6" to 12" plus! The folds that make the sheets have to retool constantly just to keep up.

## WHY DON'T STORE-BOUGHT SHEETS FIT THE BED RIGHT?

And just when they think they have it down pat and tucked away, those rascally mattress folks come out with a California King or a pillow top, or as noted in a recent Sunday paper: X-Long twin sizes to fit dorm mattresses.

Here in the Marbles household, we replaced our bed recently. The distance from top to floor increased by 2"! Our little dog found it out the hard way.

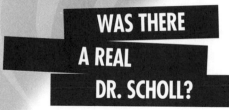
## WAS THERE A REAL DR. SCHOLL?

You bet your bunions there was!

Young Billy Scholl left farm life in Indiana and went to find his fame and fortune as a shoemaker in Chicago in the late 1800's. Realizing that shoes were causing more misery than the average foot could take, Scholl hunkered down and went to medical school. He emerged as a podiatrist—a foot doctor. His foot cushions, supports, and powders were a hit. The rest is more than a mere foot note in history.

Dr. Scholl lived well into his 80's and has over 300 patents to his credit.

Obscure fact: Foot cushions called moleskins were made out of a heavy cotton twill fabric popular at the time for trousers . . . and they did indeed resemble mole pelts.

119

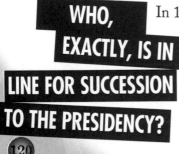

**The College of Obscure Knowledge** The order of succession has been changed by Congress four times:

The original law was passed in 1792, providing for leaders of the Senate or House to call a new election.

The law enacted in 1886 says that if both the President and Vice President are toast, the Secretary of State is next in line. After that, Secretary of the Treasury, Secretary of War, Attorney General, Postmaster General, and other Cabinet posts.

**WHO, EXACTLY, IS IN LINE FOR SUCCESSION TO THE PRESIDENCY?**

In 1947, Congress enacted the following order of succession:
Vice President
Speaker of the House
President Pro Tempore of the Senate
Secretary of State
Secretary of the Treasury

The 25th Amendment passed in 1967 gives the power to the Vice President to take over when necessary.

**WAS BABY RUTH CANDY BAR NAMED AFTER THE BALL PLAYER?**

No. However, that is a common assumption.

Actually, the bar was named for Ruth Cleveland, the daughter of President Grover Cleveland—named before the time of the Babe (the baseball player, not the daughter).

Obscure fact: Grover Cleveland was President when Babe Ruth was born in 1895.

Obscure controversy: Some claim that the candy bar was named after the granddaughter of the owners of the candy company in 1921.

Obscure monetary facts: In 1930 and 1931, Babe Ruth's salary topped out at $80,000 a year. Don't feel sorry for the guy. When you add in all the extra appearances, endorsements, and all, adjusted for inflation, his earnings were comparable to today's astronomical salaries.

At the time of this writing, I work on the 59th floor of the CitiPlex Towers, the former City of Faith building in Tulsa, Oklahoma. We get a lot of curiosities faxed in to answer in the College, such as "Do skyscrapers sway? How do the elevators work? How does the plumbing work? Why are there no bricks on the tall buildings?" So, here are the answers to the skyscraper questions!

They don't sway as much as you think—most none at all, others only inches. The secret to skyscrapers is the internal frame, as opposed to everyday external wall support.

Elevators work with cables looped around a motorized wheel attached to the car on one end, with counterweights on another.

## HOW DO SKYSCRAPERS GET WATER?

Water is pumped up to holding tanks. Vents and pipes prevent waste from plummeting to murderous velocities.

Bricks are too heavy and hard to put up and can't be seen too far up.

Obscure fact #1: The first skyscraper on a steel frame was the ten-story Home Insurance Building of Chicago built in 1885.

Obscure fact #2: New York's first skyscraper was the twenty-six story World Building in 1890.

Obscure fact #3: There are cities in the U.S. that ban skyscrapers to preserve the character of the locale—most notably Washington, D.C. and Santa Fe, New Mexico.

## WAS THERE EVER A TOOTSIE, AS IN TOOTSIE ROLLS?

Yes!

The originally hand-rolled candies were the brainchild of Leo Hirschfield, an immigrant from Austria. He named the confections for his daughter, Clara. Like most dads, he had a pet name for his little girl: Tootsie. The chewy denture-destroying candies have been popular since their introduction in 1896.

Obscure fact #1: The turn of the century was big for candy products, many of which exist to this day—such as the 1893 introduction of Cracker Jacks, who didn't put a prize in each box until 1913.

Obscure fact #2: The next round of candy introductions was in the 1940's with a Mr. Merrie and a Mr. Mars, M&M's, Milky Ways, etc.

No one really knows. I have found a dozen pages written on the matter, and no real answers emerge. It's just a clash of an ancient product being matched to a new product, and they are just now catching up with each other.

Sausages, or wieners, have been around forever—at least ever since butcher shops wanted something to do with leftovers. Hot dog buns, as we know them, have only been around for a few years. Most likely you have heard this story: At a large fair or exposition, a vender selling sausages needed something for customers to hold the hot wieners on. (Evidently this must have been a primitive society long before our current anything-on-a-stick mentality.) Suddenly a baker comes up with the idea of a bun holder for the dog.

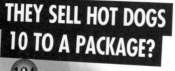

**WHY ARE THERE ONLY 8 HOT DOG BUNS IN A PACKAGE WHEN THEY SELL HOT DOGS 10 TO A PACKAGE?**

Let me attempt to answer the question. Meat comes in pounds. Ten standard dogs are a pound. Just now, bakers are catching on and making 10-pack buns. Please note that this is just as dogs are getting bigger and starting to sell 8 to a package! Sheesh!

## WHERE DOES THE TERM "EAT HUMBLE PIE" COME FROM?

This is an old saying listed in every book. This time we found literally hundreds of references all agreeing (for once!).

Humble pie is from the old umble pie which is what poor folks or servants would eat while the nobles got the good stuff. What is an umble? Here's where every source had a different story, but all point to something not microwaveable or found in your local deli. All agree that umbles are innards of some sort, such as sheep intestines, or kidneys, or the edible organs of a game animal, most likely a deer. Whatever the case, it seems after a hunt that the good meat went to the boss, the rest was made into an umble pie. Over the years, umble became humble.

Obscure fact: The word *humble* comes from the Latin word *humus* meaning "earth" or "soil."

The answer lies in legislation and history.

A kilt displays a Scotsman's tartan—the colors of his clan. When most Scots were banned from wearing kilts or tartans in the Dress Act of 1746, it became a matter of fierce pride, most likely keeping the tradition alive in rituals and games to this very day.

The kilt is the Scottish adaptation of the oldest form of dress known to man. Check out the Egyptian carvings. The kilt-like skirt was the most economical, comfortable, and (until horses became the standard) the most practical clothing for men. It was standard issue for Roman soldiers, and that's probably how it got to Scotland.

## WHY DO SCOTSMEN WEAR KILTS?

Obscure fact: The bagpipe is not originally from Scotland either, but much older. Besides playing the fiddle, Nero is said to have been good on a bagpipe. (Then again, how could you tell if he wasn't?)

126

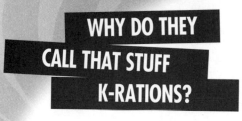

# WHY DO THEY CALL THAT STUFF K-RATIONS?

The College of Obscure Knowledge

In the war, K-rations were the only food some soldiers would see for weeks on end. Today, we would call them MRE's— Meals Ready to Eat. (Actually, it stands for something much worse, depending on the individual and the mood!)

The waxed box always contained a can of meat, a bread of some sort, gum, utensils, a dessert of some kind and, until the 1960's, a little pack of cigarettes. All in fashionable, olive green cans!

As kids, we would get these from the surplus shops to go camping. Back then we thought them great fun! Servicemen living on K-rations day after day grew tired of them really quick.

The guy who came up with the sustenance-in-a-box was a physiologist named Ancel Keys. Originally called "Key's rations," K-rations soon became the nickname.

Obscure fact: When our nation realized that the Viet Cong kept up with us eating nothing more than rice, K-rations were phased out soon after the Vietnam War for a more balanced diet.

127

**The College of Obscure Knowledge** The old story goes that English pubs and taverns had a small box to drop change into for the wait staff with the sign "to insure promptness." In later years, the saying was familiar. To cut down on magic marker costs, taverns simply put t.i.p.

Tipping as a practice has been with us for 300 years. Tipping as a necessity for income is of recent origin. Wait staff and taxi drivers, for example, depend on tips to make ends meet. This has become the standard practice in certain occupations since the Depression Era; yet, those raised during the 20's and 30's are known as the stingiest tippers.

## WHY DO WE TIP AT RESTAURANTS, AND WHO SETS THE PERCENTAGE?

The percentage is typically set by what everyone else does. Just in the last 20 years the standard 10 percent has gone to a standard 15 percent. Twenty percent is now considered the norm on the East Coast and is spreading to the big cities nationwide.

Obscure fact: Restaurants add gratuity in parties of six or more because, unfortunately, nearly always a group will stiff a hard-working wait staff as they pool their money.

# HOW DO HORSES SLEEP STANDING UP?

Horses can go months without laying down due to the inner structure of their legs.

They position each leg accordingly. They then lock up the bones and tendons, and the rest of the horse relaxes—much like a folding card table. Of course, you periodically see horses laying down, but that tends to make the muscles sore and put too much weight on the bottom lung. There are even instances of horses remaining standing after their deaths!

Obscure fact #1: A horse is classified as an odd-toed ungulate like a rhinoceros because scientists describe it as having only one toe—what we call the hoof.

Obscure fact #2: Horses have only one stomach. Grass and other forage is processed in an appendix-like holding area called a cecum that can hold ten gallons!

I got stumped on this one!

My dad (in what I assumed was a loving manner) often called me a hon-yock when I acted up or was unruly. I had honestly assumed it was a creation of his until a student of the college said his dad called him a hon-yock, too. Thus began a fruitless search. Alas, no source anywhere had it listed.

**WHY ARE ROWDY KIDS CALLED A HON-YOCK?**

I went on the radio show with it and had several similar answers that I will now use as printed fact. Due to the fact that my dad spent part of his childhood in Arkansas, he probably picked this up from the local vernacular. I am convinced that it is a Southern-Cajun-Creole conglomeration of some word that in the distant past meant something like renegade.

# WHAT IS THE DIFFERENCE BETWEEN IRAN AND PERSIA?

This question came up when a listener to the College recently re-read Hal Lindsey's *Late Great Planet Earth*.

Originally published in 1970, Lindsey lists nation by nation how he sees Biblical prophecy falling into place. One of the items mentions Persia which he states is modern-day Iran.

When the book was written, the Shah was in power. They were a strong United States ally and American businesses and tourism were thriving there. Lindsey states: "This writer believes that significant things will soon be happening there. Within a few years, came the fall of the Shah, the rise of the Iatolla, hostages, terrorism, the Gulf War, and as I am writing a new sanction embargo against Iran and Iraq by the U.S.!"

Research indicates Persia is indeed Iran. Early traders got the name from an early province, Pars, much like we identify the old Soviet Union with Russia. In the 1930's, indigenous peoples said they preferred the native Iran to the oriental-sounding Persia.

Employers throughout the ages have come up with the most creative ways to say, "You're outta here!" Some of the terms have been: fired, discharged, dismissed, booted, dumped, canned, given your walking papers, and (the latest incarnation) downsized!

Common suggestion for the phrase "getting the sack" refers to medieval craftsmen who carried their tools, lunch, and clothes in a sack. A bag or sack was the common early box or container. Getting the sack is gathering up your belongings and hitting the road. Others disagree saying craftsmen would not leave their tools of trade around to be sacked.

**WHEN YOU GET FIRED, WHY DO THEY SAY YOU GOT SACKED?**

Some suggest the figurative sacked as in an individual being pillaged or plundered. I believe the best suggestion says sacking was a common means of execution—much like bagging a criminal.

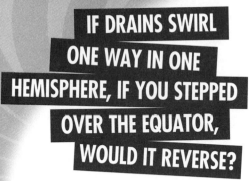

## IF DRAINS SWIRL ONE WAY IN ONE HEMISPHERE, IF YOU STEPPED OVER THE EQUATOR, WOULD IT REVERSE?

The College of Obscure Knowledge

Everybody's a comedian. The answer is no.

It's a bit of a misunderstanding that we all got from science class. We were told that due to the Coriolis effect, water drains counter-clockwise in our Northern Hemisphere.

The Coriolis effect, as described by Frenchman Gaspard De Coriolis a century ago, gives us two great truths. Great truth #1: Due to the spin of the planet, bit-time motion tends to move as described above (e.g., the hurricane and stuff like that!).

Great truth #2: Mr. De Coriolis wanted a great truth named after him.

Obscure fact: Some studies have shown that water tends to remember motion for quite a while depending on how it was poured in. (And . . . if you remembered how you got in, it's easier to get out!)

Plain old obscure truth: Our drains swirl one way or another mainly due to gravity and the shape of our drain pipe.

133

Yes, and maybe.
There really is
quicksand, but it is not the stuff you see in
Tarzan movies.

Quicksand is super-saturated sand suspended in water. Usually, it is over a spring or ample amount of water, and the sand is fine and round. It will not support weight. It will not suck you in either! However, struggling will tend to dig you in deeper because there is no air in the sand—just water. All the experts say to stay calm and use slow-motion swimming movements to get horizontal, roll your way out, clean up, then embellish the story for generations yet unborn.

## IS THERE REALLY QUICKSAND, AND CAN IT KILL YOU?

Obscure fact: More dangerous than quicksand is the soft-soap texture of an alkali bog—formed the same way, but having soft soils or clay instead of the buoyant sand.

134

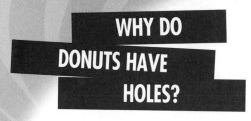

## WHY DO DONUTS HAVE HOLES?

When it comes right down to it, there are just three ways to cook dough. You can bake it, boil it (like bagels), or fry it.

Doughnuts were originally little balls of dough dunked in hot fat. Yummy. Not too far from the hushpuppies, or fried biscuits of today. They were a mainstay of the American diet from colonial times through the 1800's up until heart disease was discovered in the 1930's.

The little balls of lard-cooked batter were okay, but if you wanted it cooked all the way through, it couldn't be too big, or you would get crust on the outside and doughy on the inside. So, new ways of frying bread were born: flatten it out like Indian fry bread, drizzle in the mixture like funnel cakes, or put a hole in it!

Ta da! Donuts as we know them were born. Even today, bakers prefer immersion cooking, and the hole assures consistency.

135

The College of Obscure Knowledge

Don't repeat that question to a real chef! You'll end up sliced and diced and made into Julian fries. One reason, it's called a toque. Main reason: the chef earned it! A true, trained, professional chef is far more than just a cook. He is a supervisor of a kitchen, skilled in everything from creation to presentation.

The tradition of the headgear stems from eighteenth century France, as an identification of vocation. Like today's fast-food paper caps, sanitary keep-that-hair-outta-my-food reasons. The stiff part and the billowy top evolved later. Theory has it that the hats are high to provide ventilation for hot working conditions. Present-day toques are symbols of pride, much like the similarly impractical Shriner fez.

## WHY DO CHEFS WEAR THAT HIGH, FUNNY HAT?

Obscure fact: The word *chef* comes from the same root source as the word *chief*.

# WHY DO DOGS EAT STANDING UP, WHILE CATS LIE DOWN?

This is, of course, a generality. We have a dog that not only uses both paws to hold a bone, but rolls on its back as if eating a cob of corn in a hammock.

The answer is basic to the inherent makeup of each animal. Dogs are scavengers. Cats are hunters. Mull over that thought a second, and it will suddenly answer most questions about the behavior of your pet.

Dogs, the scavengers, are opportunistic. They beg while you eat. They eat whatever is dropped. They eat like there's no tomorrow and tend to protect with a snarl something they really like chewing on.

Cats, the predators, are patient. They eat what and when they feel like it. They happily wait until you leave to trash the place. Like their big African cousins, they are solitary creatures and don't have to worry about the rest of the pack eating more than their share.

True! No turkey, no dressing, no rolls, no butter. The early Thanksgiving feasts bore little resemblance to the Norman Rockwell-type spread we all chow down on today.

The Pilgrim governor, William Bradford, wrote his own little history called *Of Plimoth Plantation*. From that we find there were lots of venison and corn, some green vegetables, and fruit. One of my sources says the Pilgrims shunned lobster, thinking they were big insects.

**IS IT TRUE THAT THERE WAS NO TURKEY AT THE FIRST THANKSGIVING?**

Governor Bradford's journal says he sent four men fowling and they secured wild Turkeys. These were not the butterball gobblers we know, but guinea fowl. (Bet they were tough to carve.)

Obscure historical note: There were 56 Pilgrim men and 91 Indian men. These men were all served by four Pilgrim women and two teenage girls—all the women that were left alive out of the original 19 women. (I'll bet they had to clean up while the guys watched football, too!)

## HOW DO TELEPHONE CORDS TANGLE BY THEMSELVES?

This being a pet peeve of mine, and finding no answers in any reference material, a careful study of human beings (e.g., some of my coworkers) solved the mystery.

YOU are the culprit. Yes, you!

The largest percentage of us are right-handed. Now go to the phone and pick up the receiver. If you are right-handed, you used your right hand. In every phone conversation, we invariably hand-off the handset to the left hand and left ear. You have just done the twist. A dozen or so phone calls, and it is coiled like a ruined slinky.

Obscure fact: There are more holes in the mouthpiece of a telephone handset because we always hold our ear close but rarely talk directly into the mouthpiece.

Obscure note: New technology makes this unnecessary. Usually, cell phones have tiny holes to speak into.

I loved Pop Rocks! For the uninitiated, Pop Rocks were candy that exploded in little pops when mixed with saliva in your mouth.

They were taken off the market. But, no, the rumor is not true about an accident taking place. We love rumors in our country! We all became devastated when we heard the rumor that the Beatles had lost Paul. Paul is dead, we heard. Wrong. Then we heard the rumor that Jerry Mathers, Beaver from the classic television series "Leave It to Beaver," had died in Vietnam. Wrong. Then came another false rumor that the adorable kid from the Life Cereal commercials, Mikey, had passed on—due to Pop Rocks exploding in his stomach when mixed with soda pop. Wrong.

## WHAT EVER HAPPENED TO POP ROCKS?

The truth? Pop Rocks didn't survive because fearful (and gullible) parents kept their kids from buying them. Life Cereal responded by putting the now-grown-up Mikey on the cereal box, proving he was alive and well!

Obscure comeback: With little fanfare, Uniconfis Corp of Atlanta has re-introduced Pop Rocks. You can now get them at your local store once again.

## IS IT TRUE THAT ONLY HORSES AND HUMANS SWEAT?

Absolutely not.

According to the *Grolier Multimedia Encyclopedia*, one of the characteristics of being a mammal is sweat glands. Humans and horses are the most obvious examples; however, we tend to get drenched due to heat, humidity, and don't forget public speaking!

Dogs even have sweat glands, but they don't help the pups to cool off much. They're found on the paws and nose. Dogs cool off by panting but are susceptible to heat and can die in a very short time in a hot car.

Obscure fact: Pigs, like humans, have skin that can sunburn!

Obscure unrelated fact: Armadillos are the only animal other than man that can contract the skin disease leprosy.

Obscure historical fact: Sweatshops were so named after a turn-of-the-century phrase for low pay: "sweating a living."

*The College of Obscure Knowledge* It was an evil conspiracy by tie manufacturers!

The truth? Father's Day started about the same way and at about the same time as Mother's Day. In 1909, Mrs. John Bruce Smart Dodd of Seattle was moved listening to a Mother's Day sermon. She thought of her father, William Jack Smart, a Civil War veteran who raised six kids as a widower. President Woodrow Wilson endorsed the idea, but the all-male Congress didn't jump on it like they did Mother's Day. It wasn't officially designated a holiday until 1972—by President Richard M. Nixon.

## HOW DID FATHER'S DAY ORIGINATE?

Obscure Father's Day facts: Americans spend $20,000,000 a year on ties for Dad. More than 1,000,000 electric shavers are bought by little shavers for Dad. More collect calls are made on Father's Day than on any other day.

## IS IT TRUE THAT TYPEWRITER KEYBOARDS ARE DESIGNED TO BE TOUGH?

The familiar arrangement called QWERTY—due to the top row of letters—was contrived by the inventor of the first production typewriter, Christopher Scholes. Scholes and his brother designed the keyboard in 1860 to prevent jamming of equipment by proficient typers.

Before this time, letters were in alphabetical order. To add insult to Carpel Tunnel injury, those rascals marketed the QWERTY arrangement as the most efficient use of hands while typing—when the opposite is true.

Obscure fact: In 1932, after vast improvements were made to the typewriter, August Dvorak of Seattle came up with the DSK (Dvorak Simplified Keyboard) that makes the keyboard efficient to the human hand. Unfortunately, it never caught on! (Why, in today's world of non-mechanical keyboards, we continue to use the old setup is the ultimate mystery.)

Walk through any supermarket, and you'll see certain similarities. You nearly always walk through the produce first, the candy at the checkout stand, even the cereal aisles and soup arrangement looks familiar in most every store. Now ask yourself, *Why do I always seem to buy more than I came in for?*

Nearly everyone comes in to buy milk. That's why dairy is as far as possible from the front door—so you will pass by and pick up all the other stuff! That's why you are funneled through the profitable produce. That's why you see the meat when you emerge from every aisle. That's why specials are on the end of the aisles. Note: Not all is sinister conspiracy. It is also simply good common sense to stock the cold stuff along the perimeter.

## WHY ARE MEAT AND DAIRY AISLES ALWAYS IN THE BACK OF THE STORES?

Obscure fact: The most expensive and profitable goods are eye level. Look higher or especially lower for best buys!

Obscure dirty trick fact: High sugar kids' cereals are kids'-eye-level.

144

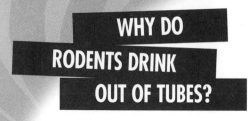

## WHY DO RODENTS DRINK OUT OF TUBES?

We humans taught them to.

It is out of custom more than anything that some pets get a bowl of water, and our caged friends get a bottle inverted with a tube. They really don't care. But you might. Water not only means sustenance, but a pool . . . or worse. One of my sources says laboratories started the trend of using a tube due to sanitary conditions. Then the good idea caught on.

That very same sanitary consideration is leading to bottled water for nearly all animals in close quarters. Pet stores and kennels are finding cats and dogs adaptable to the sipper tubes. And it's a lot nicer than dealing with spilled or soiled water bowls.

Obscure fact: Forty percent of all mammals are rodents. (So much for us being the dominant species!)

Obscure scary fact: Not all rodents are small. Beavers are rodents, and so are capybaras that grow up to 110 pounds!

You may have heard that XMAS is crossing out the Christ in Christmas. Or that at best, it is a modern, vulgar abbreviation.

Wrong, on both counts.

Xmas has been in use from the beginning of the celebration of the birth of Jesus Christ. And in case you don't know Him personally, Christ is not His last name, but a description. The term *Christ* means "the Messiah", or "the Anointed One." Christ in Greek begins with the letter *chi*: X.

## WHERE DID XMAS COME FROM? AND, IS IT BAD?

The use of Xmas is written as early as the 1500's. In fact, Christianity in old and scholarly circles is written as Xianity.

It's okay to use . . . if you can explain it so as not to offend.

## WHY IS CHRISTMAS ON DECEMBER 25?

December 25th was originally *Dies Invicti Solis*, translated "Day of the Invincible Sun" to celebrate the sun god Mithra. This day coincided with *Saturnalia*, giving homage to the god of crops, Saturn. This time was a big deal with feasting, dancing, and everything else you've come to expect from a pagan holiday.

For the first three centuries of Christianity, no one really cared about the Nativity. The Resurrection was the focal point. But when the Early Church began replacing secular hootenanny's with holy days, they figured that the sun god thing had to go. So it was decreed in the 300's A.D. No one really knows the date I guess. Every source looked up had a different date: 2336, 337, 350, and 354.

Obscure fact: *Yule* is an old Norse word for a 12-day celebration.

147

Leave it to modern technology to open this fresh wound in the battle of the sexes: the woman sits there gritting her teeth while the man clicks, clicks, clicks endlessly, pausing only for a gunfight, touchdown, or a car crash.

Several theories abound: Comedian Jerry Seinfeld says it's because men are hunters. I personally thought it was due to the fact that men hate to wait.

## WHAT IS THE DEAL WITH MEN AND REMOTE CONTROLS?

The problem is basic human nature! You hear it in every marriage seminar and in every book written about the sexes; men respond to visual stimuli, women to emotions. Ladies want to get into the story line. Guys tend to want to see something happening.

Obscure fact: A "Consumer Reports" survey said men hog the remote 38 percent to women's 15 percent. Furthermore, 85 percent of men do that annoying channel surfing.

## HOW DO THEY COME UP WITH THOSE NAMES?

Every large company has a marketing department. It is their job to come up with a name for their product so wonderful and unique that it won't get lost in the shuffle. Here is a collection of the most asked and/or most obscure:

EX-LAX: an abbreviation of "excellent laxative"

SPAM: spiced ham or sp-ham

REEBOK: a fleet-footed African gazelle (Impala was taken.)

OREO: originally the cookie was rounded; *oreo* means "hill" in Greek

XEROX: another Greek word; *xerography* means "dry writing"

No! Some humans have been rumored to eat liver, oyster, spinach, and raw fish. But goats, like people, draw the line at some point.

Goat's innards do have bacteria and stomach acid similar to Sigourney Weaver's *Aliens*, so they can eat just about anything organic—e.g., paper or material.

Obscure facts: There is no such thing as tin cans! Tin is much too expensive to use! Our cans today are mostly aluminum, or steel, or a combination of low-cost alternatives. The white you sometimes see inside cans is enamel coating to enhance coloration of contents.

**DO GOATS REALLY EAT TIN CANS?**

Obscure historical facts: Early tin cans were sealed with lead . . . poisoning. And in some documented cases they drove mad those who relied on them for food.

# WAS THERE EVER A WHITE ELEPHANT?

The College of Obscure Knowledge

I know of a velvet painting that has made the rounds every Christmas during white elephant gift parties in my church.

A gift that cannot be refused, or you cannot get rid of, and you cannot possibly keep goes back to the story of the King of Siam (yes, you may envision Yul Brynner here). The king, or emperor of what is now modern-day Thailand, would bestow a sacred albino elephant to some poor sap, who could not get rid of it (and insult the king), could not work it or even ride it (it was, after all, sacred), and eventually was driven to financial ruin.

Historically, there is no record of this happening. The closest incidence (a probable source of the saying) is 1629 A.D. when the beleaguered Charles I of England was given an elephant and five camels by the emperor of Siam. They were evidently unwanted and very expensive to maintain.

*The College of Obscure Knowledge*

St. Nicolas rode his donkey for about 1,500 years delivering gifts to children. Then, preceding all inventors and aviators, he took to the air in 1809. That's when Washington Irving under the pseudonym Diedrick Knickerbocker wrote *A History of New York*. In it, Irving describes Santa flying in a wagon, dropping presents down chimneys. Evidently flying was a bit stressful, because this is the first time we have Santa smoking a pipe.

Then in 1822, Dr. Clement Clark Moore described in detail "A Visit from St. Nicholas"—the poem later known as "The Night Before Christmas." By the way, Santa obviously packed on his weight during the interval since the 1809 sighting.

## WHERE DO WE GET OUR MODERN VERSION OF SANTA?

In 1863, political cartoonist Thomas Nash drew and forever etched in our mind the modern version of Santa.

Obscure fact #1: The Pennsylvania Dutch and French celebrate New Year's Eve with a visit from Santa's brother, Bells Nichols. He actually LEAVES cookies!

Obscure fact #2: The biggest demographic in the number of Santa believers is age four.

# WHY DO POLAROIDS DEVELOP IN LIGHT, AND DO WE HAVE TO WAVE THEM?

We have researched into every detail on how an instant picture develops. We don't understand a bit of it. We're tempted to say its MAGIC, and not for us mere mortals to know. Here goes nothing. . . . Each Polaroid print is a wonder of 17 layers of dyes and chemicals. You snap the picture. The camera squeezes the print through a roller—breaking open and mixing the goop causing chemical reactions. While the color dyes seep up from the bottom, making the picture, an alkali dye on top protects the rest from light. The exact process, chemicals, dyes, and all are secret and protected by a mountain of patents.

Today's Polaroids are quite advanced from the past. Remember the old peel-em-off prints? And that tube of pink stuff that looked and smelled like melted Chap Stick? Polaroid figures some guy thought waving the developing print would speed up things. Someone saw him do it. And like a bunch of monkeys, we all flap Polaroids for no real reason at all.

Yes! The most familiar story has Martin Luther awed by the brilliance of stars shining through an evergreen as the reason we bring in a tree and decorate it for the holiday.

There is an earlier legend you may not have heard. This one has St. Boniface (sometimes called the Apostle of Germany) rounding up some tree-hugging Druids in the 700's and giving them the facts about Christmas. During this discourse, he chopped down a good-sized oak to prove it was not sacred (talk about your sermon illustrations!). The felled tree smashed all the foliage in its path except one small fir sapling. Seen as a miracle, small fir trees were planted during Christmas from then on in Germany.

**ARE THERE TWO LEGENDS OF THE CHRISTMAS TREE?**

What I can't explain are those aluminum trees with rotating color wheels we put up in the 60's.

## WHY ARE CHIPS PRE-PRICED AT THE STORE WHEN NOTHING ELSE IS?

Did you know there's a war going on in your grocery store? The war is for shelf space! Meat, dairy, and produce provide about half of a store's profit.

If a product turns a great profit and sells well, it gets its own aisle, like cereal. Everything else must fight for space. If your product doesn't get on a shelf, it won't have a chance to be sold.

One lower-profit item, soft drinks, offer cash incentives and freebies to get good store space. That is the answer to the chip question. Chips, donuts, and other snacks are pre-priced to save the store money. They get stale, unlike canned goods, and need manpower to re-stock and price, so the chip companies do it for them.

Obscure fact: National surveys show as many as one out of ten checkout price scans are wrong!

# ABOUT THE AUTHOR

**Jim Marble's** hard-to-remember real name is Marable, the grandson of New Mexico homesteaders, and has spent the last decade in love with the people of Tulsa, Oklahoma while dreaming of the mountains back home.

Jim Marbles has been in broadcasting since the Earth cooled, and men were mindless, barbaric animals in paisley and bell-bottoms. Though a morning show host by nature, he has also been a TV weatherman, gameshow host and co-host of Southwest Showcase of Homes. Along the way, he has picked up such commendations as morning man at "Billboard Magazine Country Station of the Year" for two years in a row, "Best of Albuquerque", "Best of Tulsa" and was one of three nominees for Oklahoma Broadcaster of the Year 1994.

He walked away from the bottomless pit of despair and stress that is secular radio to return to his first love, Christian broadcasting, in mid-1994. He was fortunate to sign on with a meteorically-rising, home owned station, KXOJ, that was named by *Religion and the Media Quarterly* as the nation's Contemporary Christian Station of the Year in 1996.

His is continually peeved by people coming up to his wife of 18 years and saying "you poor thing—how do you put up with him?" His wife, Georgi, is a retirement center administrator, and both are cultivating premature gray hair due to their teenage son Jonathan.

Jim Marbles has no spare time, but if he had, would enjoy archeology, channel surfing and construction projects. He currently is an accomplished artist whose works are displayed almost entirely on his mother's refrigerator.

If you have an interesting question or would like to write the author, address your correspondence to:

Jim Marbles • P.O. Box 552 • Jenks, Oklahoma 74037

or your e-mail to: jimmarbles@aol.com.